Motorbooks International Illustrated Buyer's Guide Series

Illustrated

BUYER'S ★ GUIDE™

All New Edition

D0771889

John Heilig

First published in 1997 by Motorbooks International Publishers & Wholesalers, 729 Prospect Avenue, PO Box 1, Osceola, WI 54020 USA

Motorbooks International books are also available at discounts in bulk quantity for industrial or sales-promotional use. For details write to Special Sales Manager at the Publisher's address

Library of Congress Cataloging-in-Publication Data Available

ISBN 0-7603-0290-1

On the front cover: MG's TC virtually defined "sports car" for Americans in the period immediately following World War II, while the hardtop MGB/GT made for civilized year-around motoring. Anthony D. Henkels owns the TC and Doug Wochna the 1971 B/GT. *Dave Gooley*

On the back cover: Top: J-Type Midgets were important models for MG. In fact, a J.2 was the first MG raced in the United States, in 1934, with Barron Collier, Jr., at the wheel. **Bottom:** Many enthusiasts consider the MGA the most handsome of MG's many attractive offerings.

Printed in the United States of America

Contents

Preface and Acknowledgments

MGs were the most popular sports cars of the early postwar period, up to 1965. The sight of a TC, or MGA, or MGB today still brings a smile to many Americans. It was the first sports car many of us drove. Indeed, it was the first *car* many of us drove, after being brought up on Detroit Iron in the 1950s.

MG, the company, started out as a whim of William Morris, then became the passion of the man assigned to run Morris Garages, Cecil Kimber. The cars Kimber had designed and built also attracted passion among their owners, who decided to bond together into the MG Car Club in 1930. From the first meeting of that group came John Thornley, who would succeed Kimber and lead MG through the postwar years.

MG thrived in the United States, where most of the three-quarters of a million of them were sold. There are thousands who proudly claim to have owned or driven MGs in their past (truth be told, there are probably more claimers than MGs). MGs are still being raced and rallied and autocrossed in the United States today, even though the youngest among these cars is 16 years old. This is a tribute to the basic simplicity of the cars and their overall strength, although the bodies were prone to rust 10 minutes after they left the showrooms. My MGA was so easy to work on that a novice could perform quality tune-ups and repairs.

This *Illustrated MG Buyer's Guide* is intended to be comprehensive. It contains all the information about postwar models (and a few significant prewar models) that I was able to gather. There are, unfortunately, some holes in the data. These holes are caused by lapses in the literature, although I have done my best to confirm everything.

I used many reference sources, and they are annotated in the bibliography. Of particular value was my collection of *Safety Fast* magazines from the mid-1960s, when I was a member of the Northern New Jersey Centre of the MG Car Club. It was because of *Safety Fast*, and the fact that I was too cheap to pay full price for a subscription, that we began the New Jersey Centre of the club, which is still in existence today, some 35 years after it was begun. In my contacts with club members since the publication of my last MG book, I have found them to still be as dedicated to the car and the marque as they were 30 years ago.

Proof of the MG's popularity can be seen in this array of MGBs, MGB/GTs, and MG Midgets behind the factory in Abingdon ready for export.

In MG's modern history, more than 75 percent of its cars were exported, or more than 500,000 vehicles.

Besides the books and magazines listed, I am indebted to many people who contributed to this project. First of all, thanks must be given to Zack Miller of Motorbooks International, who first suggested the project, then prodded me until it was finally delivered. I must also thank Dave Holt, my former rally partner, who drove me all over northern New Jersey in his MGB in search of the elusive trophies. We won a few times and it was fun. In addition, thanks to Matt Stone who edited at least two versions of the manuscript and made suggestions, deleted redundancies, and asked pertinent questions that greatly contributed to the final manuscript.

Thanks also go to the owners of the various cars pictured, and to the sources of the ads. I thank Rob Van Syckle, George Iacocca, Mike Jones, Sis and Bob Eschleman, Wade Cruse, Terry Kozo, Lance Babbit, Pete Ernst, Bob Hulhouser, and Art King.

But most of all, I must thank my wife, Florence, and our wonderful daughters Susan, Sharon, and Laura for all their support and love.
—*John Heilig*

★★★★	18/80 Mark I
★★★★	18/80 Mark II
★★★★	K.1 Magnette
★★★★	K.2 Magnette
★★★	N-Type Magnette
★★★	14/28
★★⌐	F-Type
★★⌐	L-Type
★★⌐	SA
★★	J-Type Midget
★★	P-Type Midget
★★	M-Type
★★	VA

Before It Was Time For T And Some Time After

MG, the company, began as a manufacturer of sporty custom bodies on Morris chassis. In fact, the company was a captive of Morris Motors itself, being named Morris Garages for the location where the cars were built. William Morris, who became Lord Nuffield in 1934, saw the need for something more sporty than the utilitarian cars that were his bread and butter. It is to his good sense and foresight that we owe the legend of the MG, the marque.

Morris began his career as a bicycle repairman at the age of 16 in a shop behind his parents' house in Cowley, Oxford, England. This was in 1893 in Victorian England, a time and place so very foreign to what we know now. Young William was forced to leave school and get a job because of his father's failing health. His father had been forced back to England from Canada when his father-in-law became blind and could no longer farm the family property.

Morris soon branched out into building custom bicycles, primarily to satisfy the local vicar, who was so lanky he required a taller frame than was then available. In 1903 Morris began adding small engines to these bikes to create motorbikes. Then, following the path trod by so many pioneers in the auto industry, he began performing automobile repairs and then selling automobiles, after a short stint as manager of the Oxford Automobile and Cycle Agency.

By 1910, he had made his second move from his parents' home, to Oxford. He was investigating suppliers of the various components needed to build his own automobiles. Morris, an early believer in what would later be called "outsourcing," hoped to purchase as many parts as possible and manufacture as few as necessary to keep his costs low and benefit from the latest engineering advances.

Morris lacked the financial resources to begin such an enterprise, however. In 1911, the Earl of Macclesfield agreed to invest £4,000 in the business, and W.R.M. Motors Ltd. was founded in 1912.

Morris bought his engines and gearboxes from White and Poppe; his axles from

The 14/28 Tourer was the first car to wear an MG badge. It was based on a Morris Bullnose, so named because of the rounded radiator shell. An MG badge was placed just below the Motometer at the top of the radiator. About 400 of these vehicles were built. *Plain English Archive*

The car often referred to as "Old Number One" by MG purists was not, in fact, the first MG. It was a special trials car that was ordered by Cecil Kimber, seen here driving the car. Kimber used the car successfully in several trials and sold it. It was later recovered, restored, and presented to Kimber by MG employees. *British Motor Industry Heritage Trust*

E. G. Wrigley; metal artillery wheels (those with wooden spokes) from Sankey; and bodies from Raworth of Oxford. He assembled these cars in a former military training college that had once also been his father's grammar school. He called his facility The Morris Garage until 1913, when it was renamed The Morris Garages.

Morris and Hans Lanstad, the chief draftsman from White and Poppe, sailed to the United States in 1914 to check out Ford Motor Company and find out how the company could make cars so cheaply. When they visited the Continental Motor Manufacturing Company in Detroit and found they could buy Continental engines for about a third of the cost of the White and Poppe units, they returned to England with Continental's blueprints. White and Poppe couldn't match the price, so Morris and Lanstad returned to the United States in August 1914. On the way, the two set the basic design parameters for the Morris Cowley.

After ordering 3,000 engines from Continental, Morris returned to Britain and, in 1915, announced the Continental Cowley, as the car was renamed. Powering it was a 1,495-cc Continental Red Seal engine.

Unfortunately in September 1915, Chancellor of the Exchequer Reginald McKenna imposed a 33.3 percent duty on all imported goods, including automobile engines. This caused Morris' car prices to rise sharply and forced him into developing his own engines, after only 1,500 Continental Cowleys had been assembled.

Kimber's car was a 14/28, meaning it had 14 taxable horsepower and 28 real horsepower. An evolution of that car was the 14/40 Mark IV (shown here), which had similar specifications to FC7900 but had better handling because of its half elliptic rear springs in place of three-quarter elliptic springs. *Plain English Archive*

When Continental told Morris that they no longer intended to produce the engine, Morris acquired the rights and contracted with Hotchkiss to build them. In 1919, at the end of World War I, Morris began shipping his Morris Cowleys and more expensive Morris Oxfords.

The Cowley still suffered a price disadvantage to the Model T Ford. However, in January 1921, the British government imposed the Finance Act, which taxed automobiles on their RAC horsepower rating at a rate of £1 per horsepower. The big-bore Model T, rated at 22.5 horsepower, cost £23 a year in tax. The 11.9-horsepower Cowley cost only £12 a year and offered better fuel economy. This gave a boost to the Cowley's sales and kept Morris in business.

In 1922, Cecil Kimber was general manager of Morris. That year he ordered some Morris Cowley chassis and had them rebodied with custom two-seater bodies. He called the little car the Morris Chummy. When production increased, he moved his small factory to another plant in Oxford. Further sales success for the Raworth-bodied two-seaters caused yet another move, to what had been the Morris Motors radiator factory. Eventually, Kimber was able to convince Morris to set up a purpose-built factory for the construction of his two-seaters.

Succeeding the Mark IV was the 18/80 Mark II, with a 2,468-cc six-cylinder overhead cam engine. The Mark II had a four-speed transmission and was built in various body configurations. *Plain English Archive*

The 1930–31 18/100 Mark III "Tigress" was one of MG's early successful race cars. A two-door open car, the Mark III competed in the 1930 Brooklands "Double Twelve" race that ran for 24 hours, but retired after 50 laps. *Plain English Archive*

Later versions of the Chummy would provide space for a third passenger sitting over the rear axle. The Chummy rode lower than the Morris because the quarter elliptic springs used in the chassis were mounted above the frame rather than below it. Kimber also added leather upholstery.

In late 1923, the cars that Kimber was building in The Morris Garages were given the MG name. They did not wear MG badges, but they most certainly were MGs. Kimber later said that he was looking for something more distinctive than the basic Morris car when he built the Chummy.

The first car to wear an MG badge was a 1926 14/28 (14 taxable horsepower, 28 actual horsepower) that was based on a Morris Bullnose with the same horsepower designations. This car had a flat angular radiator with a nickel silver "MG" attached to it. The Bullnose radiator was also there, but the main markings had been replaced by the

MG badge. The engine was a four-cylinder side-valve unit of 1,802-cc capacity with a single SU carburetor. It had a three-speed gearbox and rear-wheel brakes in 1924. In 1925, four-wheel brakes were added. The rear suspension was by three-quarter elliptic springs, and about 400 were built.

A car revered by MG aficionados as "Old Number One," Cecil Kimber's FC7900, was not the first MG. The car was a special one-off version of a 14/28 that Kimber used to win a gold medal in the 1925 Land's End Trial. Kimber later sold the car, but it was tracked down and eventually bought back by the company.

A car that was developed from the 14/28 was the 14/40 "Mark IV," which had similar specifications, but used half elliptic leaf springs in the rear instead of three-quarters. It had better handling, brakes, and performance from its 35-horsepower engine. Approximately 700 were built.

The 1929 M-Type Midget brought MG into the sports car arena. The Midget was an angular wire-wheeled sports car that was powered by an 847-cc four-cylinder engine. The engine only delivered 20 horsepower, but the chassis only weighed 1,100 pounds, making for a lively combination. *Plain English Archive*

Next in line was the 18/80 Mark I and II, with a chassis design that was entirely by MG. Powered by a 2,468-cc six-cylinder overhead cam engine with two SU carburetors, the 18/80 was built in two-seater, four-seater, and sedan variations. The Mark I had a three-speed gearbox, while the Mark II used a four-speed box attached to the 80 horsepower engine. Half elliptic springs defined the suspension. Approximately 750 were built.

Because production had outgrown the small space allotted to him, Cecil Kimber moved the MG Car Company to a separate factory in Abingdon, about six miles from Oxford, in 1928. The factory had previously been occupied by the Pavlova Leather Company. Being separated physically from Morris, Kimber now had the independence to run the company the way he saw fit.

Despite Kimber's fondness for sports cars, MG's primary products (and money-makers) during the 1920s were generally large sedans and convertibles. One exception was the MG 18/100 Mark III, which was a pure race car, also known as the Tiger or Tigress. It was entered in the 1930 Brooklands "Double Twelve" race, where it retired after 50 laps.

The Tigress was built in 1930 and 1931. It was developed from the 18/80 Mark II and had similar specifications, with the exception of dry-sump lubrication, two spark plugs per cylinder, a close ratio gearbox, brakes that could be adjusted from the cockpit, and other variations. Only five of this four-seater open racer were built.

MG became the company we know today with the introduction of the M-Type Midget in 1929. Here was an angular wire-wheeled sports car that was unlike anything MG had built before. The M-Type was the first production MG, based on the then-current Morris Minor. Powered by an 847-cc four-cylinder engine with 20 horsepower available, it wasn't overpowering. But the engine was installed in a body that only weighed 1,100 pounds. It also offered excellent handling. One of the first major successes for the M-Type Midget was in the 1920 Monte Carlo Rally, where F. M. Montgomery broke the 1,100-cc class record in the Mont des Mules hillclimb. Approximately 3,200 M-Types were built from 1929 to 1932.

MG put a destroked and supercharged M-Type engine into a streamlined fabric body and hired George E. T. Eyston to drive it. Eyston thus became the first person to drive a 750-cc car over 100 miles per hour on February 16, 1931, when he topped 103 miles per hour at Montlhéry.

This car was the nucleus of the C-Type Montlhéry Midget, with a supercharged 746-cc engine rated at 52.4 horsepower at 6,500 rpm. The C-Type used a four-speed gearbox and semi-elliptic leaf springs. Only 43 of these cars were built, with their aerodynamic radiator shell.

MG adopted a new slogan in 1930, "Safety Fast." The company would use this slogan to define its cars for half a century.

Safety Fast meant that the MG would go fast, but it wouldn't put the driver or passenger in danger at that speed.

Also in 1930, a group of owners formed the MG Car Club. John Thornley, who was an accounting student, was named honorary secretary. Thornley joined the company in 1931 and would become its general manager in 1952.

Another development of the M-Type was the D-Type Midget, which was an M-Type with a touring body, carrying four-seater or "salonette" bodywork. The engine was the 847-cc overhead cam four that delivered 27 horsepower at 4,500 rpm. The early cars used a three-speed gearbox, but the later ones had a four-speed box. MG built 250 D-Type Midgets.

Following the alphabet (sort of), the next significant model was the F-Type Magna, built in four-seater tourer (F1 and F3) or two-seater (F2) configuration. Approximately 1,250 F-Types were built. The engine was a development of the M-Type, but with two additional cylinders, giving a capacity of 1,271 cc. This engine developed 37.2 horsepower at 4,100 rpm.

The next significant MG model was the J-Midget. The J.1 and J.2 were powered by 847-cc four-cylinder engines, while the J.3 and J.4 used a 746-cc four. The J.1 and J.2 were the most popular, with 2,500 built, compared to 22 J.3s and nine J.4s.

A J.2 was the first MG to compete in an American road race. Barron Collier, Jr., drove one in the Targa Florio race sponsored by the Automobile Racing Club of America (ARCA) on September 15, 1934. Briggs Cunningham also raced a J.2 in some ARCA events.

Next, MG built the K-Type Magnettes, which were based on a sedan chassis. The first Magnettes used a six-cylinder engine of 1,087-cc capacity with three SU carburetors. Later versions used 1,271- or 1,286-cc engines. In KA form, the engine only delivered 38.8 horsepower. But in KB form, with only two carburetors, power was up over 40 horsepower. The KC engine used a coil ignition rather than a magneto. Body styles included four-seater sedans and tourers on the long wheelbase chassis and two-seaters on the short wheelbase chassis.

Not all of the 3,200 M-Types built by MG were sports cars. Some received attractive coupe bodies, as with this 1929 sportsman's coupe. *British Motor Industry Heritage Trust*

The ultimate K-car was the K.3 Magnette. In these cars, George Eyston and Count Gianni Lurani won their class in the 1933 Mille Miglia. Tazio Nuvolari drove a K.3 and broke the class record seven times while winning the 1933 Ulster Tourist Trophy race. Sam Collier, Barron's brother, took his K.3 to Le Mans and drove in that race as well as other events on the continent. The K3 used a supercharged version of the 1,087-cc engine that was rated at 120 horsepower at 6,500 rpm.

When supercharged cars were banned from the Ulster Tourist Trophy race in 1934, MG entered an N-Type Magnette with a 74-horsepower engine. Six Magnettes were entered in the race, with one of the two survivors winning by 17 seconds.

The M-Type engine was the basis for the EX120 record-breaker. George E.T. Eyston drove this car at Montlhéry to a speed of more than 103 miles per hour. The M-Type engine had been destroked to 746 cc and a supercharger added to boost horsepower to 52.4. This was enough to allow EX120 to become the first under-750-cc car to top 100 miles per hour. *Plain English Archive*

The L-Type Magna was built in open two-seater and four-seater models, as well as a four-seater salonette and a two-seater coupe. Of the 575 built, all used a six-cylinder variation of the F-Type's 1,087-cc engine that was rated at 41 horsepower at 5,500 rpm.

For 1934, the factory racing car was the T-Type Magnette, with a twin carburetor version of the 1,286-cc engine that developed 56 horsepower. Approximately 750 were built in various body styles.

MG announced its withdrawal from racing in the middle of the 1935 season. The claim was that MG had been handicapped out of racing in England and the company would take time for the production models to "catch up with extremely advanced ideas incorporated in the present racing car, which is highly specialized and years ahead of its time."

The real reason for the withdrawal was that specialized racing cars would not be produced in the future, due to Lord Nuffield's

MG took the engine from the EX120 record-breaker and installed it in a new midget, the C-Type. Also known as the Montlhéry Midget, the C-Type used an aerodynamic radiator shell that was very un-MG-like. It had a four-speed gearbox and semi-elliptic leaf springs in the rear. *Plain English Archive*

Above and below: The J-Type Midgets were significant models for MG. J.1 (above) and J.2 (below) Midgets used 847-cc engines, while J.3 and J.4 Midgets used 746-cc fours. A J.2 was the first MG raced in the United States in 1934 when Barron Collier, Jr., drove in the ARCA-sponsored Targa Florio race. *Plain English Archive*

British Motor Industry Heritage Trust

The K-Magnettes were sedan based, which surprised some people who complained about MG's naming its postwar sedans Magnettes. The KA was modestly powered, but the K.3 Magnette, with a supercharged 1,087-cc engine developing 120 brake horsepower, powered George Eyston and Count Gianni Lurani to a class win in the 1933 Mille Miglia. A K.1 Magnette is pictured.

dislike for racing. Rather, the company would build cars using as many standard components as possible.

The production car was the PA Midget, which had entered production in 1934 with an 847-cc engine. A team of three PAs, managed by George Eyston and with all-woman driving teams, had finished 24th, 25th, and 26th at the 1935 Le Mans race. The P-Type engine was bored out to 939 cc and attached to a close-ratio transmission. It was now known as the PB Midget.

MG also had Q-Type and R-Type Midgets in the line. The Q-Type, introduced in 1934, combined the K.3 wheelbase of 94.2 inches and N-Type track of 45 inches with N-Type steering and brakes. It used K.3 bodywork and had a Zoller supercharger on its 750-cc engine. In regular tune, the engine delivered over 100 horsepower. In "sprint" form it produced 146.2 horsepower at 7,500 rpm.

However, the Q-Type soon became too fast for its chassis. An MG engineer once said, "You never see a picture of a Q-Type with all four wheels on the deck. For Brooklands, we had to fit grab-handles on the floor so that the mechanic could keep himself inside the car."

The successor to the Q-Type was the R-Type with an all-independent suspension. The engine was the Q-Type's, with modifications to strengthen it. The brakes were cable-operated drums. As with the Q-Type, the fuel tank formed the tail of the car.

MG introduced the car in April 1935. *Motor Sport* said the car was one "which will be the admiration of the rest of the world . . . a genuine Grand Prix racing car in miniature. Nothing like it has ever been within the reach of motor-racing enthusiasts for the price, either in England or on the Continent."

However, in July 1935, Lord Nuffield (he had earned his peerage in 1929) sold the MG Car Company and Wolseley Motors to Morris Motors. The racing program was put on hold and the overhead cam engines were replaced with pushrod-operated overhead valve units. The Abingdon design office was closed and transferred to Cowley.

But the most shocking change to come over MG was the introduction of the SA in October 1935. Here was a large sedan, built on a 123-inch wheelbase, that would compete with William Lyons' Jaguar SS. The engine had overhead valves operated by pushrods and a hydraulic braking system. It even had a synchromesh gearbox. Introduced as the MG Two-Litre, it had its engine enlarged to 2,288 cc before it went into production, primarily because it was now competing with the 2,664-cc Jaguar SS. The SA handled better than the Jaguar, according to some reports, but was unstable in the wet because of its great length.

MG returned to sports car production in the spring of 1936 with the introduction of the TA Midget. This car is covered in the next chapter, but suffice it to say it was a good deal better than the P-Type Midgets that had preceded it. F. Wilson McComb, in *MG by McComb*, wrote, "This new TA model was not altogether welcome to those who liked the compact dimensions and crisp behavior of the ohc Midgets; indeed, the original exhaust system soon had to be altered so that it made a little more noise! Really, MG's new smallest sports car was in effect a Magnette, not a Midget."

In 1937, MG introduced the VA-Type tourer with a 1-liter overhead-valve pushrod four-cylinder

EX127 was the record-setting K-Type. The car used a K.3 engine and exceeded 128 miles per hour in 1933. George Eyston is seen driving the car here, but the ulti- mate record was set by Bert Denly, Eyston's mechanic, when the car was rebodied and became too small for Eyston to fit in the cockpit. *Plain English Archive*

engine rated at 55 horsepower. The VA was built on a 9-foot wheelbase in sedan, tourer, and convertible bodies. It was a good seller for MG, with approximately 2,400 produced.

Successor to the SA was the WA, with a wider body and a 2,561-cc six-cylinder engine rated at 100 horsepower. Built in sedan and convertible body styles, the WA used a four-speed gearbox with the top three gears synchronized. Approximately 370 were built before the onset of World War II halted production.

Cecil Kimber remained as general manager of MG into World War II. During the war, MG produced a complex section of the Albermarle bomber. Miles Thomas, the vice chairman and managing director of the Nuffield Organization, was in favor of gearing up for military projects. He and Kimber clashed over the Albermarle contract and Kimber was dismissed in 1941. Kimber was killed in a train accident in February 1945 at the age of 59.

John Thornley, who had joined the company after the formation of the MG Car Club in 1931, was named general manager of MG in 1952 with the creation of BMC by the merger of the Morris and Austin organizations. Leonard Lord was made president of BMC, whose offices were moved to Longbridge, and Lord Nuffield was named president, which was a purely honorary position. Nuffield died in 1963.

Sydney (Syd) Enever, who was the creative force in MG design for more than 30 years, died in 1993. Enever joined MG in 1929 in the experimental department. He designed the EX135 record-breaking car that Goldie Gardner drove on the German autobahns in 1938 and 1939. Enever and Cecil Cousins are credited with the creation of the MG TD, as well as EX176, one of the MGA prototypes.

After Thornley became general manager, Enever became chief engineer. In that role he designed EX181, the Stirling Moss/Phil Hill record breaker of 1957 and 1959.

Enever's last major project was the 1962 MGB.

Collectible Value

Among the older MG models, the 18/80 Mark I and II and K1 and K2 Magnettes are considered the most valuable, followed, in order, by the N-Type Magnette, the 14/28, F-Type, L-Type, SA, J-Type Midget, P-Type Midget, M-Type, and VA.

MG in America

Immediately after World War II Zumbach in New York was responsible for importing MGs, but this was soon taken over by J. S. Inskip in New Jersey who covered the Northeast. MG distribution in the mid-Atlantic was handled by Royston out of Philadelphia; Wacky Arnolt distributed MGs in the Midwest; Ship and Shore in West Palm Beach serviced the South; Overseas Motors covered Texas; Gough Industries covered southern California; and Kjell Qvale's British Motors Distributors handled northern California. After 1953, the Hambro Trading Company, later Hambro Motors, handled all MG importing.

Morris and Austin merged in 1952, and The British Motor Corporation/Hambro,

The K.3 Magnette had a purposeful dash, with large clear instruments designed to feed information to the driver. Note there is no speedometer, just a large tachometer in front of the driver, two oil gauges for pressure and temperature, a vacuum/pressure gauge and "rad" gauge to measure the radiator's temperature. *British Motor Industry Heritage Trust*

After the K-Type, MG built the L-Type Magna in 1933/34. This continental coupe version was one of only 575 built. All used a 1,087-cc six-cylinder engine that developed 41 brake horsepower. *Plain English Archive*

Inc. was formed in January 1963 to handle distribution of BMC products in the United States. and Puerto Rico. At the time there were twelve regional distributors and 600 franchised dealers. BMC/Hambro was located at 734 Grand Avenue in Ridgefield, New Jersey, before moving to 600 Willow Tree Road, Leonia, New Jersey. Upon the

In the mid-1930s, MG offered the PA Midget with an 847-cc engine. The PB Midget (shown here) used a bored-out 939-cc version of this engine. Both the PA and PB were offered in lovely Airline coupe versions with fastback styling. The PB was also fitted with a close-ratio four-speed transmission. *Plain English Archive*

eventual dissolution of what was then the British Leyland Motor Corporation, the Rover Group took over the Leonia headquarters, then passed them on to Jaguar when Rover stopped importing cars into the United States.

At Ridgefield, there were over 8,000 square feet of office space and 65,000 square feet of warehouse. One public relations representative once told me in 1962 that there were enough parts in the warehouse to build a complete MG TC from scratch. Ridgefield was "computerized" as early as the late 1960s, the reason it ran so efficiently. The Parts Department kept track of 30,000 different items, valued at around $10 million (in 1967) and shipped $1.2 million in parts to distributors every month.

With computerized assistance, BMC/Hambro was able to forecast market trends, and place orders with the factory three months ahead of scheduled delivery, with estimates for what would be needed six months in advance.

BMC/Hambro also produced dealer sales aids and publicity material, including display ads. The Dealer Development Department produced a standardized accounting system for its dealers, established standards for used cars, showrooms and service and parts departments, and produced sales-assistance material.

Besides the parts and offices, there were facilities for rebuilding and reconditioning parts in the Service Technical Department. The SU carburetor rebuilding operation, for example, reconditioned more than 20,000 units every year, with a failure rate of less than 0.1 percent.

Graham Whitehead was in charge of the Ridgefield operation in 1967 as chief executive officer of BMC/Hambro. He would eventually lead Jaguar Cars.

MG and SS, the company that would become Jaguar, found themselves competing in the same market when MG offered the SA sedan, which was very similar to the SS sedan. The car was introduced as a two-liter and carried a 2,288-cc engine. Some reporters said the SA handled better than the SS, but was unstable in the wet. *British Motor Industry Heritage Trust*

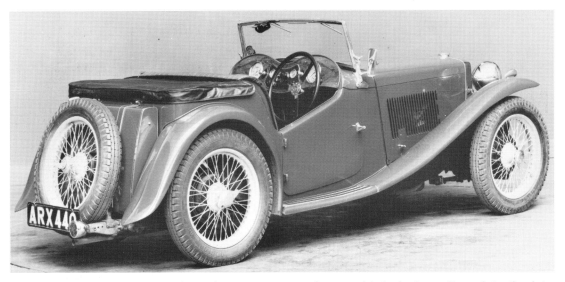

The TA, introduced in 1936, showed a return to "Midget" production for MG. Here was a sports car with then-modern styling. TA styling would, in fact, continue into the late 1940s with the TC, which was essentially the same car. *Plain English Archive*

TAs were offered with open styling and with a stylish Tickford roof, as seen here. *British Motor Industry Heritage Trust*

Chapter 2

MGT Types

★★★★(R)	★★★★	MG TB
★★★★(R)	★★★	MG TF1500
★★★★(R)	★★★★	MG TA
★★★★(R)	★★★★★	MG TC
★★★★(R)	★★★★↲	MG TD
★★★(R)	★★★	MG TF1250

Because of its rarity, the MG TB has a higher value than any other T-series MG. The TF1500 is also considered more valuable because it is the true precursor to the MGA. However, in the United States, the TC is revered almost to the point of holiness by MG aficianados, and the TF1500 is less revered. Therefore, two ratings are included for this series of cars; the relative value (R) and the normal star ratings.

Most Americans first discovered MG with the TC, which was imported in fairly good quantities after World War II. But the TC was merely a postwar version of the prewar MG TB, which had just entered production in 1939 when hostilities broke out and the company

Right after World War II, American cars were beginning to show the influence of aerodynamic design with more rounded shapes. American drivers were simply not ready for the spidery and angular MG when it began appearing on these shores. Here was a car that was vertical and showed no deference to slipping through the air.

had turned its interest to the production of war materiel.

The TB was, itself, an evolutionary step from the TA, which was a departure from the vehicles MG had been building to that time. So the T-series' history rightly begins prior to World War II and continues right up to the introduction of the MGA in September 1955.

MG TA

The TA was introduced in June 1936. MG's sporting reputation to the time had been built with the series of Midgets, and the TA was a bit larger. But while the Midgets often used overhead cam engines, the TA's four-banger was a pushrod design. But the decision to use a more traditional engine was part of a program by the Nuffield organization to make use of common components. This program was created in 1935 by Lord Nuffield (William Morris) and his managing director Leonard Lord. Lord will return to our story as managing director of British Leyland Motors, the organization that eventually saw the (near) demise of MG in the 1970s.

The engine for the TA was a 1,292-cc unit referred to as MPJG. It was made by Morris Motors Engines Branch and was based on a Wolseley 10/40. The compression ratio was 6.5:1 and it delivered 50 horsepower at 4,500 rpm. It was a long stroke design, with a bore of 63.5 mm and a 102-mm stroke. This design was chosen because of Britain's taxation policies, which rated the engine at 10 horsepower based on the bore.

Because of the inherent weakness of long-stroke engines versus short-stroke engines, the powerplant was not a strong one nor did it take well to tuning. Valve diameter was 30.5 mm for the inlet valves and 26.0 mm for the exhaust valves.

Carburetion was by two SU 1 1/4-inch semi-downdraft type HV3 carburetors. The cylindrical AC air cleaner was painted black and was located at the back of the engine compartment.

In the TA, the cylinder head was cast iron and the entire engine assembly was painted bright red, almost orange. The

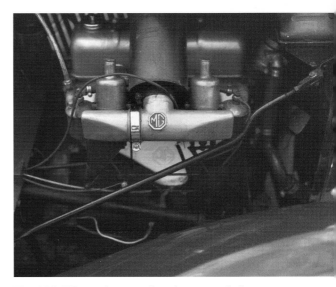

The MG TB used an engine that was similar to that in the TA, but bored out to 66.5 mm giving a capacity of 1,250-cc. It also received a new designation, XPAG. With a fully counterbalanced crankshaft, the engine's output was 54.4 brake horsepower.

aluminized three-branch exhaust manifold led to a single pipe that ran down the right side of the car through a Burgess muffler to a single exhaust pipe.

Unlike the previous MG Midgets, the TA's cooling fluid circulated with the assistance of a water pump. A four-bladed fan assisted cooling air through the radiator. On the exterior, the radiator cowl was chrome-plated and had an enamel octagonal MG badge. The radiator had an external filler cap, which was also octagonal and chrome-plated.

Radiator slats were usually painted to match the upholstery color. On the TA, the upholstery usually matched the body color, so the slats were also painted the same color as the body. Often, contrasting color upholstery was found on cream, black, and green cars, which was reflected in the color of the slats.

Right: With a body widened by four inches to create more comfortable seating, the TC was only obviously different from its predecessor from this angle. The rear seat cushions had 22 flutes, reflecting the wider body.

The MG TC had obvious prewar styling, with a vertical, slab-sided, 15-gallon fuel tank strapped on the back, 19-inch wire wheels with "motorcycle" tires, and, of course, right-hand drive, because England had not yet decided to build cars expressly for export.

With its vertical styling, the original wide 16-gallon (Imperial) fuel tank of the TA was strapped to the rear. Later TAs as well as all TBs and TCs used a narrower 13-gallon tank, also strapped to the back of the car. Both tanks had three gallons in reserve.

The first four-speed transmissions offered on the TA had no synchromesh. After engine No. MPJG/684, synchromesh was added on third and fourth gears only. The nonsynchromesh transmission had a final ratio of 3.715:1, while this was raised to 3.454:1 for the synchromesh-equipped cars.

The body for the MG TA was definitely a prewar style car, with a decidedly square appearance and a vertical grille. It was built on an ash frame reinforced by a steel framework and using plywood paneling. The body was steel. Doors were mounted by two hinges and opened from the front.

On the TA, a pear-shaped bulge on the left-hand side of the hood was there to clear the generator. It was located about halfway up the louvers. The TA also had a toolbox mounted under the hood, with the jack clipped to the front panel of the box.

The original TA body was designated B.269 and had narrow rear fenders without a central rib and the wider fuel tank. In 1937, the body changed to B.270, which had wider rear fenders and a central rib, as well as the narrower fuel tank.

Salmons and Sons built Tickford Drophead Coupe bodies on the TA and TB chassis. The first TA Tickford Drophead was built in 1938. It was the first of 260 TA Tickford Coupes. Unlike the roadsters, the Tickford had semaphore "trafficators" turn signal indicators built into the sides, just beneath the windshield.

Tickfords also had fixed window frames, instead of the fold-flat style of the roadsters. The windshield was hinged at the top and could be folded up to a horizontal

The radiator of the MG TC was identical to that of the TB. Many owners paint the radiator slats.

position. Windshield wipers were mounted on the body instead of on the windshield.

MG TA seats had a single back with two seat cushions, a unique approach to "bucket seats." Upholstery was of Connoly leather, with the backs upholstered in Rexine leather-like cloth. The TA seat had 20 flutes on the backs, with the seat cushions having 8 flutes each. The TA's dash incorporated five round black-on-white instruments. On the left, in front of the passenger,

was a 5-inch diameter Jarger speedometer. To its right were an ammeter and oil pressure gauge, both mounted in a black instrument panel. The 5-inch tachometer was mounted in front of the driver, with a water temperature gauge fitted on the far right.

MG TB

Introduced in April 1939, the MG TB was destined to have a short life. Production of all automobiles in Great Britain ceased that August when Britain declared war on Germany. In its short life, only 379 MG TBs were produced. The powerplant for the TB was an improvement over that used in the TA. With a bore increased to 66.5 mm, the XPAG engine was taxed at 11 horsepower. But the compression ratio was also increased, to 7.25:1, over the TA's engine and power increased to 54.4 horsepower at 5,200 rpm. Torque was 64 foot-pounds at 2,600 rpm. The XPAG engine had a fully counterbalanced crankshaft.

The XPAG engine as used in the MG TB was referred to as a "Group 1" engine. Engine numbers went from 501 to 883. Two styles of rocker cover were offered for the TB; a chrome-plated pressed steel type or a cast aluminum type. The oil filler cap was at the back end of the engine and the dipstick

Compared with the MGA and MGB, the TC is definitely a "vertical" car, with no concessions to aerodynamics. With a tall grille and motorcycle tires and fuel tank strapped on the back its styling hearkens back to cars of the 1930s when it was, in fact, designed.

Part of the charm of the TC was its "cycle" fenders and headlights that were not fared into the fenders, as in more modern cars. Here was a postwar car that still had the charm of many of the better prewar cars.

had an MG badge on the handle. In addition, the valves were enlarged to 33 mm for the inlet valves and 31 mm for the exhaust valves. The color was red, as with the TA engine, but it was a slightly darker color.

The exhaust manifold was a four-branch affair, since the XPAG engine had separate exhaust ports for each cylinder. After joining to a single pipe, the gases flowed through a Burgess muffler. One change from the TA was that the TB's fan was painted black, rather than red. Other radiator features were the same, except that the TB's engine had a different radiator core. The color of the slats matched the upholstery, as with the TA. Carburetion was by two SU type H2 semi-downdraft carburetors. The large air cleaner was mounted at an angle over the rocker cover between the carburetors. The TB used the same 13-gallon tank found on later TAs, still strapped to the back.

A Borg & Beck dry clutch replaced the cork-lined oil bath clutch found on the TA. The transmission also added synchromesh to second gear, as well as third and fourth. The final drive ratio was 5.125:1. Body construction was similar to that of the TA. One difference was in the location of the generator-clearing bulge in the left side of the hood. On the TB and TC, it was located near the bottom of the louvers, not midway as in the TA. As with the TA, a toolbox was mounted under the hood. It, too, had the jack clipped to the front of the box.

The body designation for the TB was B.270, with the narrow fuel tank and wider rear fenders. The TB Tickford Drophead Coupe is a rare beast. Only 60 are known to have been built. It was virtually identical to the TA Tickford, with semaphore turn signal "trafficators," fold-up windshield in a fixed frame, and windshield wipers mounted on the body rather than the windshield. The Tickfords offered rear seating and "landau" irons on the top. Seats were identical to those of the TA. The TB's instrument panel was essentially identical to the TA. As with the TA, an eight-day manual clock was at the bottom of the tachometer. The center of the panel in both the TA and TB was painted black, while in the TC it was changed to metallic tan or bronze.

MG TC

When World War II ended, and British manufacturers rushed back into production, there was no time to develop new models. Consequently, MG decided to adopt a one-model policy, with that one model based on

Tall 19-inch tires and wire wheels soon defined "sports car" for Americans. Later T-series cars and most other sports cars would go for lower-profile wheels and tires, but a trend had been set by the TC.

The front suspension of the TC was non-independent with semi-elliptic springs and Luvax-Girling piston-type shock absorbers. It didn' t provide a soft or luxurious ride, but the stiffness made for spirited handling, which was unlike anything the Americans who adopted TCs by the thousands were accustomed to.

the 1939 TB Midget. The new car was provided with a body that was 4 inches wider, and had different instruments and a simplified suspension. The leaf springs for the solid rear axle were mounted in rubber bushings, rather than sliding trunnions mounted in rubber covers. Improved Luvax-Girling shock absorbers were now used, replacing the Luvax Type AR hydraulic lever arm shocks of the TA and TB. The front suspension consisted of semi-elliptic leaf springs, with five leaves on the TA, seven on the TB, and six on the TC. Since the engine wasn't changed, many people said the TC was 10 years out of date when it was introduced.

While it was definitely not a great race car, despite its sportiness, the MG TC still had a quick release fuel filler cap, just in case some owner wanted to enter his car at Le Mans and needed to make quick pit stops.

What happened surprised everyone. The postwar world went crazy for the TC, and MG in four years sold three times as many TCs as any other car the company had offered. It wasn't great, but it was a true sports car, unlike anything seen in the United States, which was its biggest market. Race drivers learned their craft in MG TCs. Among the great American drivers to cut their teeth in TCs were Briggs Cunningham, John Fitch, Ken Miles, and Phil Hill.

The MG TC engine was the same 1,250-cc unit used on the MG TB, with a few exceptions. Most MG TC engines used a cast aluminum rocker cover that was painted silver-gray green. However, a cast aluminum rocker cover was installed between engine Numbers XPAG/2020 and XPAG/2966. The TC's XPAG engine was a "Group I" engine, just as the TB's was. Engine numbers ranged from 884 to 10,863. Radiator and exhaust features for the TC engine were the same as for the TB. The toolbox on the TC was narrower than that found on the TB, because the battery box had been located in front of it. The TC had a spare can of oil supplied, as did the TA and TB. But on the TC, there was a special holder for it on the front of the battery box.

Credit for the TC's styling goes to Sydney (Syd) Enever, who joined MG in 1930. Enever, who was described by MG historian F. Wilson McComb as "a former Morris Garages shop-boy who was to reveal a rare talent for original design," penned the T-series, many chassis and suspension components, and several of the record-breaking racers in his years with MG.

The TC's body number was B.280, which was a number created to reflect the TC's extra 4 inches between the rear door pillars. The TC also has only two tread strips

The wheels seem to tilt when you make a turn and the tires are way too tall and thin for modern driving, yet here was the car that would spark a revolution and introduce sports cars to American drivers. The TC wasn' t the best of the postwar sports cars, it was just different enough to develop a cult following.

The TC' s engine was fed by two 1 1/4-inch SU semi-downdraft carburetors. Most MG TC engines used a cast aluminum rocker cover that was painted silver-gray-green. Cast aluminum rocker covers were installed between engine numbers 2020 and 2966.

on the running boards, while the TA and TB have three each. Seats were essentially identical to those of the TA and TB, except the rear cushion had 22 flutes, because of the wider body. Instruments were the same as with the TA and TB, with the exception that the clock at the bottom of the tachometer was now electric. What appealed to the Americans who fell in love with the TC was its "motorcycle" tires and wheels; 4.50x19-inch tires on 2.50x19-inch wheels. As one writer put it, the TC was the last of the cart-sprung square-riggers from Abingdon.

It was also the first MG built after the end of World War II. It was the first sports car many Americans had even seen or driven. *Safety Fast* magazine published an essay by an American writer that called the TC "four-wheeled noise that's fun to drive," which accounted for its popularity in the United States. Here was a car that looked like no American car, yet could out-accelerate and out-handle any of them. The difference between the cars soon disappeared, and better sports cars were soon available, but the TC had gained a stronghold.

MG TD

While the TC was clearly a derivative of the prewar cars, the TD, introduced in 1949, was a concession to modernity. While it wasn't nearly as aerodynamic as the contemporary Jaguar XK120, for example, it still had a prewar character in a slightly more modern body.

The TD's chassis was a completely new design, unlike the TC that preceded it. The

29

The Americans who bought MG TCs were surprised by the instrument panel. A tachometer was in front of the driver, rather than a speedometer. All the accessory gauges were mounted in the center of the dash. This arrangement would have been practical for a manufacturer who produced right-hand and left-hand drive cars, but the TC was available in right-hand drive only.

TD's wheelbase was 94 inches, the same as the TC. But the TD used more conventional 4Jx15-inch wheels and 5.50x15 tires. With larger tires on smaller diameter wheels, the overall view of the TD was less vertical than the TC.

Between the front wheels was a strong, box-section cross-member that carried the independent front suspension, the steering gear, front engine mounts, and the radiator. The engine was the same 1,250-cc engine as in the TC, still rated at 54 horsepower at 5,400 rpm. The engine drove the rear wheels through a four-speed manual transmission with synchromesh on the top three gears.

The TD's engine was a "Group I" XPAG engine, with engine numbers that went from 501 to 9407. Some "Mark I" TDs used a "Group II" XPAG engine that was labeled XPAG/TD/2 and went from engine numbers 9408 to 17968. "Group III" XPAG engines were installed on later TDs, with engine numbers 17969 to 30290. The difference between the Group I, II, and III engines is that parts may be exchanged within the Groups but often parts may not be exchanged among Groups. Heads and blocks in Group III, for example, are different from the earlier ones and must be mated together.

The rare TD Mark II used an XPAG 1,250-cc engine that was essentially the same as that which would appear in the TF 1250. These XPAG engines were labeled XPAG/TD/C. Alec Issigonis designed the TD's front suspension, which was all new to sports cars but first used on the Y-Type sedan. It was a design that would live through the last MGB.

MG made concessions to aerodynamics with the design of the TD, which was lower and softer than the angular TC. Part of this design shift may have been because of the shift to "automotive" rather than "motorcycle" tires and the resultant lower profile.

With a totally new chassis and body design, the TD was more modern than the TC, but it still retained some of the "square rigger" styling of its predecessor. Part of the reason for the lower profile was the 15-inch wheels, four inches less in diameter than the 19-inch wheels of the TC.

The coil-and-wishbone design had a lower wishbone mounted in rubber-bushed bearings on the chassis. A plate between the arms of the wishbone carried the coil spring, whose top rested in a "cup." The upper wishbone was the lever arm of the hydraulic shock absorber.

In the rear were conventional semi-elliptic leaf springs with seven leaves. These were mounted in rubber-bushed bearings on the outside of the chassis. Steering was by rack-and-pinion, with the mechanicals borrowed from the Y-Type sedan. The steering column was telescopically adjustable, and the steering wheel was 16 inches in diameter. Brakes were hydraulic drums, with twin leading shoes at up front .

The TD (and later TF) was fitted front and rear with full-width chrome bumpers with pointed ends. Ribbed bumper overriders were also fitted. A hole for the crank starter was located in the center of the front bumper. Both the TD and TF used an Auster windshield, secured with Phillips screws for the first time. Both models also had plain tread plates at the bottom of the doors, with no company name.

TD and TF tops were made from biscuit-colored canvas with the frame painted a light tan. The TD originally used a two-bow frame similar to that of the TC, but a three-bow frame was fitted on later models. The three-bow design was carried over to the TF.

With the three-bow top, sidescreen design was also changed. Early sidescreens had a top that sloped down toward the rear. With the three-bow design, the top and bottom lines of

From the rear, the MG TD shows more flowing lines. Under the after-market luggage rack is a fuel tank that is less vertical and gives a more flowing look to the rear end. Disc wheels, rather than the wire wheels of the TC, were also a concession to practicality because of the difficulty of keeping wire wheels "in tune."

the plastic in the sidescreen were parallel, and the top line of the rear sidescreen was at a steeper angle. TF sidescreens are different from TD screens because of the steeper rake of the windshield.

The TD did not achieve many significant competition successes; it was recognized as an outdated car from the outset. However, a works team did finish one, two, three in the 1950 Tourist Trophy race, and George Phillips drove a rebodied TD in the 1951 Le Mans race. While this wasn't the MGA prototype that some claim, it was significantly more aerodynamic than the stock TD. Engine trouble led to the car's retirement from the race.

MG TF

By 1953, the TD had been in production for more than four years and there wasn't much more that could be done to the model. The prototype MGA had been shown, but production was delayed. MG was in desperate need of an interim model, since the TD's lines were getting old quickly and the XPAG engine didn't offer a lot of power.

Enter the MG TF.

While the TF has been scoffed at by many historians, it was a true interim model for MG. In its styling, it offered a transition between the TD and A, and in the engine compartment, the A's 1,488-cc engine would be first used in the TF.

For styling, the body was lowered and the radiator shell was canted back for an overall lowering of 3 inches. The hood picked up a definite slope, which made the car look sleeker. In addition, the front fenders were restyled and the headlights were faired into

ARNOLT MG

While the TD didn't make any aerodynamic waves, it was the source of two interesting models: The chassis formed the underpinnings for the prototype of what would become the MGA and the semi-custom Arnolt-MG.

Legend has it that Stanley Harold "Wacky" Arnolt II, the Chicago-area distributor for Morris and MG, visited the 1952 Turin automobile show, where he was stricken by a pair of Bertone models, a coupe and a cabriolet, built on two-year-old MG TD chassis. Nuccio Bertone had spent his last lire on the chassis and the exhibit was a life-or-death proposition for him. They were all he had left.

Bertone was at his stand when a tall man in a Stetson cowboy hat, high-heeled cowboy boots, rich suit, and silk tie tapped him on the shoulder. "I like your cars," the cowboy allegedly said to Bertone. "I want you to build me a hundred of each."

The cowboy was Wacky Arnolt, who had made his fortune building 20-horsepower engines to power tenders and lifeboats for the thousands of boats built during World War II. After the war he bought an MG TC, loved it, and immediately opened an imported car showroom to sell everything from MGs to Aston Martins and Rolls-Royces. He eventually became the Midwest BMC distributor.

Arnolt met with Bertone after the Turin show, then left for home. On the way, he stopped at Abingdon and arranged for 200 chassis to be shipped to Turin for Bertone to build into Arnolt-MGs. As it would turn out, Abingdon only shipped 100 chassis, 65 coupes and 35 cabriolets. MG switched from the TD to the TF in October 1953 and the TD chassis simply wasn't available any more.

Bertone took over a year to build the 100 cars. He then shipped them to the United States. Later Arnolt became the U.S. distributor for other Bertone cars.

The Arnolt-MG used the same 94-inch wheelbase as the TD, but was 150 inches long, compared to 145 inches for the TD. It incorporated the traditional MG grille in a two-plus-two body with a decent trunk. With better aerodynamics, the top speed of the Arnolt was about 90 miles per hour, compared to 80 miles per hour for the TD. The price was $3,145, compared to less than $2,000 for the TD.

Later, Wacky Arnolt would commission the Arnolt Bristol, which was loosely based on the Bristol 404, which was loosely based on the BMW 328. Rene Dreyfus would manage the Arnolt-Bristol racing team that finished one, two, four in the 1955 Sebring 12 Hours under-two-liter class.

---

them, much like a Pierce-Arrow of the 1930s. At the back, the fuel tank also received a pronounced slope to match the front. Another concession to modernity was the removal of the windshield wiper motor from the top of the window frame to under the hood.

Inside, octagonal instruments appeared for the first time in a T-series, although octagonal bezels had been used on the WA sedan and N-Type Magnette, and were mounted in the center of the dash for left-hand or right-hand drive. The instrument panel was tilted forward under a padded safety roll.

Tom McCahill, dean of American automotive journalists, said of the MG TF in *Mechanix Illustrated*: "I feel the new TF is a big disappointment . . . Mrs. Casey's dead cat slightly warmed over. To get down to facts, the new MG TF is a dyspeptic Mark II imitation that falls short of being as good as the Mark II. . . . Only out of supreme arrogance would the manufacturers attempt to keep ramming this old teapot down the throats of American buyers."

It wasn't that easy to get to the engine because only the top of the hood would open, unlike the clamshell opening hoods of

Some of the charm of the TD is lost when the top is raised. While the car could be fun in the open air, it was slightly cramped with the top up. Plastic side curtains are not installed in this view.

the TC and TD. And the radiator wasn't real, as in the older cars, but a false front with a dummy filler cap. Inside, though, there was more room in the cockpit and the passengers sat in true bucket seats.

Early MG TFs used an XPAG engine labeled XPAG/TF and ran from engine numbers 30309 to 36330. These were "Group III" XPAG engines.

Effective July 1954, the later MG TF 1500 used an XPEG engine, with engine numbers ranging from 501 to 3940. The new engine gave better performance, as much as five additional miles per hour, and better acceleration.

Tuning the T-series Engines

The XPAG 1,250-cc engine used in the

From the front, the TD's grille is far less vertical than that of the TC, giving the car a lower look.

Grilles could be chrome or painted the same color as the body.

TB, TC, and TD was amenable to tuning. With a base compression ratio of 7.25:1, it could be raised to 8.6:1 by removing 3/32 inch from the cylinder head face. Polishing the inlet and exhaust ports and other minor machining should increase output to around 60 horsepower.

Stage 2 tuning of the XPAG engine begins with grinding away another 1/8 inch from the gasket face of the cylinder head, increasing the compression ratio to 9.3:1. Adding larger valves with 150-pound valve springs and grinding away the valve seats will increase power to 66 horses. Tuning up to Stage 4 will result in a 75-horsepower engine, while adding a Shorrock supercharger will boost it to 97.5 horsepower. However, all XPAG engines are 45 to 50 years old at best, and any tuning for performance should be undertaken with the greatest of care.

THE AUTOCAR ON MG

Britain's *The Autocar* magazine was quick to review the MG models as soon as they appeared. The magazine's comments on the various T-series models are interesting.

TA: "On the road, the 'feel' of the car has undergone a change; the new Midget is softer, quieter, and more flexible at low speeds from the ordinary touring car angle. No car, even a sports machine, is driven fast all the time, and to be able to potter really satisfactorily is a quality worth having." September 18, 1936

TB: "There is no sideways 'give' when cornering fast, and the steering, though light, is nicely accurate and firm, but the springing is a great improvement for comfort over the old types. You notice the difference between various kinds of surfaces, and feel fairly appreciable movement over the less good, but never real shock." June 28, 1940

TC: "Always one has the feeling of being able to make a fast run easily in the [MG], for it responds so readily to all the controls and is so quick—eager, it seems—to get moving. The biggest factor in this and other directions, apart from the actual performance available, is the complete sense of command which the driver feels he has over the car at all times, including the major features of brakes, steering, and road holding on corners." October 17, 1947

TD: "The feel of the car on the road inspires confidence and there is the impression that even an indifferent driver could make a good showing behind the wheel; however long the journey, the actual driving of the car is beguiling all the way." May 15, 1953

TF: "The MG Midget is a car that, probably, has changed less in outward appearance than any other model over the same period of time, and it is this feature that makes the car contrast so sharply with the production models of overseas countries, such as the United States of America. . . . Over the years, the model has been developed to improve its performance, handling qualities, and general comfort." October 16, 1953

Early MG TDs used a "Group 1" 1,250-cc XPAG engine. In total, three different "groups" of XPAG engines were used on the TD, with parts that could be exchanged within groups but not among them.

Right: The concept of individual bucket seats had still not appeared in the TD. However, unlike its predecessor, there was a small cargo area behind the seats that was big enough for a briefcase.

The XPAG engine in the MG TD used twin SU carburetors, type H2. Group 3 engines used type H4 carburetors. All are 1 1/4-inch throat of the semi-downdraft variety.

New with the TD was an independent front suspension consisting of wishbones and coil springs. Luvax-Girling or Armstrong lever-action shock absorbers completed the package. This essential design would continue through the MGB.

Compared with the front fender of the MG TC, the TD's fender line is softer and more flowing. This would be the last MG with bullet-style headlights unattached to the fenders.

This MG TD was still built in the era of the MG Car Company. In later years, MGs would be built by the British Motor Corporation, British Motor Holdings, and finally, by the British Leyland Motor Company.

Introduced in 1953, the MG TF was lower and more aerodynamic than the TD that had preceded it. Conceived from the beginning as an interim car between the TD and MGA, which had already been introduced, the TF had a style that harked back to the TC era but gave a taste of what was to come.

The first thing you saw on the TF was, of course, the grille. It was smaller than the TD's and, in fact, was a false grille, used as a styling touch to conceal the real radiator. This owner has added after-market fog lights and club badges.

Wire wheels were an option on the MG TF and are popular among restorers. Tire size was 5.50x15, the same as the TD.

Instruments in the TF reflected an MG heritage. They were octagonal and located in the center of the dash. The location was ideal for a company that would manufacture both right-hand and left-hand drive cars. Another advantage was that the driver and the passenger each had glove compartments.

TF instruments included a tachometer closer to the driver and speedometer closer to the passenger. The central octagon included a water temperature gauge, ammeter, and oil pressure gauge. Jaeger manufactured the instruments. The pull knobs are for the choke and starter and control airflow into the cockpit.

This manufacturer's plate identifies the car as an MG Series "TF." From the serial number we can tell that it is a 1955 MG TF1500 with the larger engine.

Clamshell-opening hoods may be handsome, but they make servicing the engine difficult. Adjusting the needles on the twin SU type H4 carburetors was a challenge.

Chrome rocker covers and air-cleaner covers were not standard on the MG TF. While they do brighten the engine compartment of the car in this over-restoration, they are not authentic.

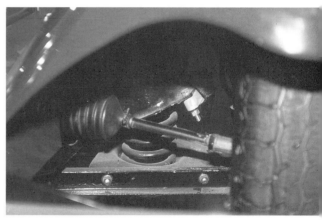

The TF used the same front suspension as the TD: dual wishbones and coil springs with Armstrong hydraulic lever-action shock absorbers.

Specifications

MGTA

Production dates: 6/36–4/39
Total production: 3,003 (2,741 two-seaters, 2 Airline coupes, 260 Drophead Coupes)
Chassis numbers: TA/0253–TA/3253
Engine numbers: MPJG
Price: $1,205
Engine:

Type: Cast iron inline four cylinder
Displacement: 1,292 cc
Bore: 63.5 mm
Stroke: 102 mm
Compression ratio: 6.5:1
BHP: 50 @ 4,200 rpm
Torque: N/A

Transmission

Type: Four-speed Nuffield-type manual
Clutch: Cork, single oil immersion plate
Overall gear ratios:

		To Engine 683	After Engine 683
4th*	1.00:1	1.00:1	
3rd*	1.42:1	1.32:1	
2nd	2.20:1	2.04:1	
1st	3.72:1	3.45:1	
Reverse	3.72:1	3.45:1	
*Synchromesh			

Rear axle ratio:

To Engine 683	After Engine 683
4.89:1	4.89:1

Chassis:

Type: Open-channel side members with five tubular box cross members
Wheels and tires: 2.50x19 wire
Tire size: 4.50x19
Brakes: Lockheed hydraulic 9-in drums front and rear
Front suspension: Beam axle, semi-elliptic springs, hydraulic lever-action shocks
Rear suspension: Live axle, semi-elliptic leaf springs, hydraulic lever-arm shocks
Steering: Bishop cam, worm and peg
Electrical: Two 6-volt batteries
Fuel system: Twin SU type HV3, semidowndraft
Fuel tank: 15 gal
Dimensions:

Wheelbase: 94.0 in
Overall length: 139.5 in
Track front: 45.0 in
Track rear: 45.0 in
Width: 56.0 in
Height: 53.0 in

Curb weight: 1,764 lbs (Drophead 1,960 lbs)
Colors:

        Exterior: Saxe Blue, Coral Red, Apple Green, two-tone green, maroon, light gray, black, Metallic Gray
        Interior: Gray, maroon, biscuit, brown

Significant chassis modifications:

        After engine 684: Synchromesh on third and fourth gears
        After chassis TA/2253: Centralized chassis lubrication system installed

MGTB

Production dates: 5/39–10/39
Total production: 379 (319 two-seaters, 60 Drophead Coupes)
Chassis numbers: TB/0253–TB/0629
Engine numbers: XPAJG501–XPAG883
Base price: $1,205 (est.)
Engine:

        Type: Cast iron inline four cylinder
        Displacement: 1,250 cc
        Bore: 66.5 mm
        Stroke: 90 mm
        Compression ratio: 7.25:1
        BHP: 54 @ 5,500 rpm
        Torque: 65 ft-lbs @ 3,400 rpm
        Red line: 5,700 rpm

Transmission:

        Type: Four-speed manual
        Clutch: Single dry plate, Ferodo
        Overall gear ratios:

                4th*   1.00:1
                3rd*   1.36:1
                2nd*   1.95:1
                1st   3.38:1
                Reverse 3.38:1
                * Synchromesh

        Rear axle ratio: 5.125:1

Chassis:

        Type: Open-channel side members with five tubular box cross members
        Wheels and tires: 2.50x19 wire
        Tire size: 4.50x19
        Brakes: Lockheed hydraulic 9-in drums front and rear
        Front suspension: Beam axle, semi-elliptic springs, Luvax-Girling shocks
        Rear suspension: Live axle, semi-elliptic leaf springs, Luvax-Girling shocks
        Steering: Bishop cam, worm and peg
        Electrical: Two 6-volt batteries
        Fuel system: Twin SU H2 semidowndraft carburetors
        Fuel tank: 15 gal
        Dimensions: (same as TA)

Wheelbase: 94.0 in
Overall length: 139.5 in
Track front: 45.0 in
Track rear: 45.0 in
Width: 56.0 in
Height: 53.0 in
Curb weight: 1,736 lbs
Colors: (Same as TA)
Significant chassis modifications:
After TA/2253: Centralized chassis lubrication system installed

MGTC

Production dates: 11/45–12/49
Total production: 10,000
Chassis numbers: TC/0252–TC/10251
Engine numbers: XPAG884–XPAG10863
Base price: $2,238 (1947)
Engine:
Type: Cast iron inline four cylinder with pushrod-operated overhead valves
Displacement: 1,250 cc
Bore: 66.5 mm
Stroke: 90 mm
Compression ratio: 7.25:1
BHP: 54.4 @ 5,500 rpm
Torque 65 ft-lbs @ 3,400 rpm
Red line: 5,700 rpm
Transmission:
Type: Four-speed manual with synchromesh on top three gears.
Clutch: Single dry plate, Ferodo
Overall gear ratios:
4th*   1.00:1
3rd*   1.36:1
2nd*   1.95:1
1st   3.38:1
Reverse 3.38:1
* Synchromesh
Rear axle ratio: 5.125:1
Chassis:
Type: Box section steel with tubular cross members
Wheels and tires: 2.50x19 center lock wire
Tire size: 4.50x19
Brakes: Lockheed hydraulic 9-in drums front and rear
Front suspension: Beam axle, semi-elliptic springs, Luvax-Girling piston-type shock absorbers
Rear suspension: Live axle, semi-elliptic leaf springs, Luvax-Girling piston-type shock absorbers
Steering: Bishop cam, worm and peg
Electrical: One 12-volt battery
Fuel system: Twin SU H2 type 1 1/4-in semidowndraft carburetors
Fuel tank: 15 gal

Dimensions:

        Wheelbase: 94.0 in

        Overall length: 139.5 in

        Track front: 45.0 in

        Track rear: 45.0 in

        Width: 56.0 in

        Height: 53.0 in

        Curb weight: 1,764 lbs

Colors:

        Exterior: Black, MG Red, Shires Green, Sequoia Cream, Clipper Blue

        Interior: Regency Red, Vellum Beige, Shires Green

Significant chassis modifications:

        Engine 884: Introduction of timing chain tensioner

Driver's Handbook factory part number: AKD663

Parts List factory part number: AKD856

MGTD

Production dates: 11/49–8/53

Total production: 29,665 (28,643 TD, 1,011 Mark II)

Chassis numbers: TD/0252–TD/29915

Engine numbers: XPAG/TD (501-9407), XPAG/TD/2 (9408-17,029), XPAG/TD3 (over 17,029)

Base price:$1,850 (1950)

Engine:

        Type: Cast iron inline four cylinder

        Displacement: 1,250 cc

        Bore: 66.5 mm

        Stroke: 90 mm

        Compression ratio: 7.25:1, 9.2:1 on TD/3 engine

        BHP: 54 @ 5,400 rpm

        Torque: 65 ft-lbs @ 3,400 rpm

        Red line: 5,700 rpm

Transmission:

        Type: Four-speed manual

        Clutch: Single dry plate, Ferodo

        Overall gear ratios:

                4th*   1.00:1

                3rd*   1.39:1

                2nd*   2.07:1

                1st   3.50:1

                Reverse 3.50:1

                * Synchromesh

        Rear axle ratio: 5.125:1

Chassis:

        Type:

        Wheels and tires: 4Jx15 bolt-on discs

        Tire size: 5.50x15

        Brakes: Lockheed hydraulic 9-in drums front and rear

        Front suspension: Independent with wishbones and coil springs, Luvax Girling or Armstrong lever-action shocks (Mk II had additional friction shocks)

Rear suspension: Semi-elliptic leaf springs, Luvax Girling or Armstrong lever arm shocks

Steering: Rack and pinion

Electrical: One 12-volt battery

Fuel system: Twin SU, H2 type carburetors, H4 on TD/3

Fuel tank: 12 gal

Dimensions:

    Wheelbase: 94.0 in

    Overall length: 145.0 in

    Track front: 47.4 in

    Track rear: 50.0 in

    Width: 58.7 in

    Height: 53.0 in

    Curb weight: 1,932 lbs

Colors:

    Exterior: Black, MG Red, Almond Green, Ivory Clipper Blue, Autumn Red, Sun Bronze

    Interior: Red, beige, green

Significant chassis modifications, beginning with:

    Engine XPAG/TD/501: Modified flywheel with 93 teeth, 10 on starter pinion

    Engine XPAG/TD/6482: Different type water pump

    Engine XPAG/TD/7576: Oil pickup moved to a central position in the sump

    Engine XPAG/TD/9008: Modified rockers installed, requiring the use of different spacers

    Engine XPAG/TD/2/9408: A larger diameter clutch was introduced, which necessitated a different type of flywheel

    Engine XPAG/TD/2/10900: A shorter dipstick guide tube was introduced

    Engine XPAG/TD/2/14224: A combined filter and oil pump was introduced

    Engine XPAG/TD/2/14948: A larger capacity sump was fitted

    Engine: XPAG/TD/2/17289: Shorter push-rods were added, as well as longer adjusting screws

    Engine XPAG/TD2/17969: Revised passages in the head and block required a different type of gasket

    Engine XPAG/TD2/20972: A priming plug was incorporated in the oil pump

    Engine XPAG/TD2/24116: The "softer" camshaft of the Y-engine was introduced

Driver's Handbook factory part number: AKD618E

Workshop Manual factory part number: AKD580A

MGTF

Production dates: 10/53–2/55

Total production: 9,600 (6,200 MGTF, 3,400 MGTF Mark II/MGTF 1500)

Chassis numbers: 501–10100

Engine numbers: XPAG/TF/30309–XPAG/TF/36330; XPEG 501–XPEG3940

Price: $2,195 (1954); $1,995 (1995 TF1500)

Engine:

    Type: Cast iron inline four cylinder

    Displacement: 1,250 cc 1,466 cc

    Bore: 66.5 mm 72 mm

    Stroke: 90 mm 90 mm

Compression ratio: 8.0:1
BHP: 57 @ 5,500 rpm 63 @ 5,000 rpm
Torque: 65 ft-lbs @ 3,400 rpm 78 ft-lbs @ 3,000 rpm
Red line: 5,700 rpm
Transmission:
Type: Four-speed manual with synchromesh on top three gears
Clutch: Single dry plate Ferodo
Overall gear ratios:

4th*	1.00:1
3rd*	1.39:1
2nd*	2.07:1
1st	3.50:1
Reverse	3.50:1
*Synchromesh	

Rear axle ratio: 4.875:1
Chassis:
Type: Box-section steel with tubular cross-members
Wheels: Bolt-on pressed steel. 4Jx15
Tire size: 5.50x15, 6.00x15 optional
Brakes: Lockheed hydraulic 9-in drums front and rear. Two leading shoes front
Steering: Rack and pinion
Front suspension: Independent by coil springs and wishbone. Armstrong hydraulic shock absorbers
Rear suspension: Semi-elliptic leaf springs, interleaved with rubber and rubber mounted Armstrong hydraulic shock absorbers.
Electrical: One 12-volt battery
Fuel system: Twin SU, H4 type, 1-in carburetors
Fuel tank: 12 gal
Dimensions:
Wheelbase: 94.0 in
Overall length:147.0 in
Track front: 48.2 in
Track rear: 50.3 in
Width: 59.75 in
Height: 52.5 in
Curb weight: 1,932 lbs
Colors:
Exterior: Black, MG Red, Almond Green (MG Green), ivory, Birch Gray
Interior: Red, green, biscuit
Significant chassis modifications:
After TF/1501: High pressure fuel pumps fitted
After TF/3495: Piston dampers added to carburetor dashpots
After TF/6887: Wire wheel designs changed to incorporate a deeper-dished inner flange
Driver's Handbook factory part number: AKD658A
Workshop Manual factory part number: AKD580A
Parts List factory part number: AKD804
Special Tuning Manual factory part number: AKD654

Chapter 3

MGA

★★★★★	MGA Twin Cam Roadster
★★★★↙	MGA 1600 Mark II DeluxeRoadster
★★★★	MGA Twin Cam Coupe
★★★★	MGA 1600 Mark I/Mark II Roadster
★★★	MGA Roadster
★★★	MGA 1600 MarkII DeluxeCoupe
★★★	MGA 1600 Mark I/Mark IICoupe
★★	MGA Coupe

The above relative values are based on reports in several publications. The top three cars are all either the Twin Cam or are Twin Cam-based with the Deluxe chassis. Later MGA models, such as the 1600 Mark I and Mark II, rate higher than the 1,500-cc engined car, even though an "original" MGA still has high collector value.

The MGA was the most popular sports car of its time. It was the best-selling sports car ever, until the advent of the MGB, which was eventually knocked from the list by the Chevrolet Corvette and Mazda Miata. The MGA in all its guises was the epitome of the British sports car. It had sleek lines that were a distinct departure from the square-rigged T-series cars that preceded it. It had progressively better engines that were responsible for improved performance. And while it had lever shock absorbers and a solid rear axle, it still offered excellent handling that was unmatched by anything Detroit could offer at the time.

And it was cheap. You could buy an MGA for anywhere from $2,195 to $2,706 ($3,550 if you include the Twin Cam coupe) through the life of the car. The car offered more fun per dollar than anything available then or now. After building essentially the same shape sports car for 20 years—the square-rigged MG T-series—the time had come for a complete breakaway. The T-series cars had charm, but the trend was toward higher speeds, and the Ts couldn't enter this arena because of their square and decidedly nonaerodynamic shape.

The MGA body was a further development of a streamlined body designed by Syd Enever to fit on the TD chassis. It was called EX172 and was developed for the 1951 24 Hours of Le Mans race. George Phillips drove the car in the race and it retired after three hours with a broken valve spring. Despite being a prototype and a race car at that, the car was well finished. The interior had fitted carpets, padding around the door edges, and a telescopic steering wheel that would follow the car through its life. The driver's seat was well upholstered and the body even included a cut-out in the door for the driver's (right) elbow. In the rear was a faired-in license plate light, while just behind the driver's head was the quick-release fuel filler.

Up front, there was a hint of what the eventual MGA grille would look like. It had a chrome frame around a series of vertical slats. And while in final dimensions it resembled what the MGB was to look like more than the MGA, because of its flatness, the idea was there. The transition had been made from the vertical grilles of the T-series. The next evolutionary prototype was EX175, with a design dated February 20, 1952. This car was an obvious extension of EX172, with a longer wheelbase and different fender treatment.

This is the car that began it all for the author, a 1955 MGA 1500. When this picture was taken in 1960, it had to share a parking space with my roommate's 1957 Chevrolet Bel Air coupe, a car that would eventually establish a stronger passion than the MG.

MG planned to produce EX175 as the next MG sports car. These plans hit a snag when the Nuffield organization merged with Austin Motors to form British Motor Corporation in 1952. Leonard Lord was in charge of policy control and John Thornley was general manager of MG.

Thornley recalled that the MG engineers met with Lord (who had once worked for MG) and showed him the MGA prototype. They were three days too late, because Donald Healey had approached Lord earlier with the proposal for a 2-liter four-cylinder sports car that would eventually become the Austin-Healey 100. Lord recognized that the two cars were very similar and squelched the MGA. MG would have to do with the MG TF as an interim model.

Development of the MGA continued, however, with another prototype, EX182, which was the MGA in its final form. Production was finally approved in June 1954, with an introduction date of April 1955 set. The MGA was formally introduced to the public at the Frankfurt Auto Show on September 22, 1955. It was called the A because MG had gone through the alphabet with the Z-Magnette sedan and was starting over. The first MGA was built on May 27, 1955, and bore chassis No. 10,101, which followed after the last MG TF chassis No. of 10,100.

The engine for the MGA came from the ZA Magnette sedan, tuned to sports car specifications. The engine and car were tested exhaustively at the 1955 Le Mans and Tourist Trophy races. Production began in August 1955.

MGA 1500

MGAs were available in three basic versions, four if you count the Twin Cam. All were based on engine enlargements with

The MGA was a good car for competing in gymkhanas. In this event, held in a National Guard armory, the author tries his hand at weaving between the pylons. Gymkhanas of the time were a less expensive (and safer) method of going racing. The modern equivalent is a time trial or field trial.

minor body changes added to differentiate the models. The initial model, introduced in 1955, was known simply as the MGA (later as the MGA 1500) and was equipped with the 1,489-cc (90.8 cubic inches) unit that was a carryover from the MG TF.

The BMC "B" engine used in the production MGA 1500 was similar to the engines used in the Le Mans racers, but detuned for road use. Carburetion was the same, with twin 1-inch SU carburetors. In addition, the compression ratio was reduced from the 9.4:1 of the racers to 8.3:1, and there was a modified camshaft, which was designed to give a lower horsepower and torque peak speed. Horsepower, then, was reduced from the 82.5 at 6,000 rpm of the racers to 72 at 5,750 rpm after starting out at 68 horsepower at 5,500 rpm. This same basic engine was also used in the Austin A-50, Morris Oxford, and MG ZA Magnette.

Because the engine was not of the cross-flow design, and the intake and exhaust

The classic rear fender line of the MGA has never been duplicated. While it resembled the Austin-Healey and Jaguar XK120, the MGA's fender line would remain essentially unchanged for eight years, as would the general profile of the car.

ports were siamesed, the cylinder head was probably the weakest part of the engine design. Hot spots would form at the siamesed exhaust ports between the second and third cylinders, which often resulted in cracked heads. Cross-flow heads were available in the after-market.

Unlike the T-series cars, the MGA was also available as a coupe, with wind-up windows and locking doors. Coupe versions of all the various MGA models were available. The first coupe appeared in October 1956 at the London Motor Show. They offered more civilized motoring at no loss of performance, because the improved aerodynamics of the permanent hardtop made the car faster.

MGA Twin Cam

After the 1500, the next iteration of the MGA was the MGA Twin Cam, introduced in July 1958. The 1,588-cc double overhead cam engine had problems, despite the fact that it delivered great performance and had the potential for becoming a great engine. One Twin Cam owner I knew back in the 1950s was famous for leaving the company parking lot and chirping the tires in all four gears.

It is important to check the ignition timing of the Twin Cam engine often. Later Twin Cam engines had a lower compression ratio, which reduced the tendency for piston failure due to poor timing.

Safety Fast, the MG Car Club publication, said, "In the right hands the Twin Cam was a splendid and exhilarating car to own, but the high-efficiency engine did not, alas, take kindly to neglect; mixture strength, octane rating, and ignition timing had to be just right, while the engine revved so freely that, in indirect gears, it could be blown up in a moment by mere carelessness—the tachometer was there to be used, but not every owner appreciated this."

After the end of the Twin Cam production run in June 1960, several chassis (the exact number is unknown) were left over. Since there were no more Twin Cam engines to install in the chassis, they were used first with 1,588 and then 1,622-cc engines and designated 1600 Deluxe and 1600 Mark II Deluxe. Like the Twin Cam, these Deluxe

The MGA was a simple car, perhaps one of the last of the simple cars. An example of that simplicity is the clean instrument panel. In front of the driver were the important instruments, tachometer and speedometer. To the right was the fuel gauge. In the center was a radio speaker grille with the horn button located underneath. The radio was optional. And since this was before the era of "smart stalks," the turn signal switch is located to the left of the tachometer. It clicked 22 times then self-cancelled.

Grilles such as these allowed engine heat to escape. They were located on each side of the hood, and identified the car as an MGA. Later versions included a "1600 MK II" or "Twin Cam" to identify the models that followed.

The MGA was the first MG sports car with true "bucket seats." The driver and passenger each had a contoured back to the seat with separate seat cushions, separated by the transmission tunnel. This car is equipped with an after-market wood steering wheel.

models had four-wheel disc brakes, center-lock steel disc wheels with knock-off hubs, and Dunlop 5.90x15 Road Speed tires.

MGA 1600

The next generation MGA was the MGA 1600, with an enlarged version of the engine, bored out to 1,588 cc (96.9 ci). This car delivered 78 horsepower at 5,500 rpm, just six more than the engine in the 1500. But torque increased from 77 foot-pounds at 3,500 rpm to 87 foot-pounds at 3,800 rpm, which was a significant increase. Since the Twin Cam had already been introduced, the 1600 was a practical compromise, with horsepower and torque curves lying nicely between those of the 1500 and Twin Cam. The MGA 1600 also had disc brakes up front and improved drum brakes in the rear.

John Thornley said in *The MG Companion* that the company was thinking of giving the MGA a facelift, if only to lure potential buyers into the showrooms. But, as Thornley said, since "the MGA is an idealized design, conceived as an entity, it is hardly surprising that no matter what we did to the front, the result was less satisfactory, and usually less aerodynamic. Instead, the company tried to analyze what MGA users wanted most, and the answer came back, "better performance," which translated as "more power." Consequently, very little was done to modify the shape of the body, except to conform with new regulations, and the modifications went into the engine compartment.

MGA 1600 Mark II

The final iteration of the standard MGA was the 1600 Mark II, with a 1,622-cc version of the trusty BMC four-banger. This engine proved to be the most powerful and reliable of the three in the group, with 90 horsepower

The MGA was as simple as they come, with classic aerodynamic styling that set it apart from the T-series cars that had preceded it. The cars were susceptible to rust, however, particularly in the rocker panels below the doors and at the seam between the rear fender and the side panel. Rust could also develop between the headlight and turn signal light.

at 5,000 rpm. Torque increased to 97.5 foot-pounds at 4,000 rpm. Top speed was in the neighborhood of 105 miles per hour, depending on who was doing the testing.

While displacement was increased, primarily by increasing the bore by 1/32 inch to 3.0 inches, there were significant internal changes to the engine as well to improve power. The cylinder head was modified to improve gas

flow and higher compression, increased from 8.3:1 to 8.9:1. Flat-topped pistons were used to increase the compression ratio, replacing the dished pistons used in the older engines. Intake and exhaust valve diameters were increased by 1/16th inch, the volume of the combustion chamber was increased, and the quality of the valve steel was improved.

All MGA engines up to the 1600 Mark II were equipped with crank starters, "just in case." These were some of the last cars in the world to be so equipped. If the batteries failed to start the car, the crank could be employed. That was, unfortunately, a more frequent occurrence than with other cars because the batteries were located under the car, behind the rear seat. Bombarded by road muck, the clamps could lose good contact with the posts. The location of the electric SU fuel pump, outside next to the fuel tank on the right side, also posed problems. The pump would stop working if it got wet, even though the contacts were covered with a rubber boot. Driving an MGA in wet weather was always a challenge.

Gearbox

All the engines were linked to a four-speed manual gearbox with synchromesh on the top three gears. It seemed as if MG was

This factory MGA 1500 prototype has the optional wire wheels and luggage rack, as well as a nonstandard hood that may have been a cover for a different engine at the factory. Note the absence of exterior door handles. The "knock-offs" on the wire wheels would be legislated out of existence by federal safety laws.

An interesting press kit photo, since no self-respecting woman in a fine business suit would wear that outfit to ride in an MGA. The MGA was designed for jeans and casual clothes, even though many business people used the cars as daily commuters.

Right: The MGA 1600 was identical to the original MGA, except that the engine capacity had been increased from 1,489 cc to 1,588 cc. Power also changed from 68 brake horsepower to 80 brake horsepower. To distinguish a 1600 from the 1500, look at the marking on the air vent which includes a "1600" next to the oval. Two-piece taillights also replaced the one-piece units of the original.

Poetry in motion!

Soar into a new world of your own in the MGA '1600'. There's nothing quite like the way its swift new horses level the hills and the way it steps through tight bends with cat-like precision. And there's a gratifying feel of solid safety when its new disc brakes take command. No matter what you've been driving—no matter what it cost—you owe it to yourself to test-drive the new MGA '1600'. Call your BMC dealer and name the date today! And...ask him to tell you about the full 12 months' factory warranty.

Safety- MG *fast!*

BEST KNOWN SYMBOL OF WHAT
A SPORTS CAR SHOULD BE

Free literature and overseas delivery information on request.

A product of **THE BRITISH MOTOR CORPORATION, LTD.**, makers of Austin-Healey, Austin, MG, Magnette, Morris and Riley cars.
Represented in the United States by HAMBRO AUTOMOTIVE CORP., Dept. SCI, 27 W. 57th St., New York 19, N.Y.
Sold and serviced in North America by over 1,000 distributors and dealers.

forever wedded to the notion of not having synchromesh on first gear, because it was well into the life of the MGB before it was introduced. The MGA 1500 gearbox was the same as on the Magnette and incorporated a close pattern with short shifts. Top speeds in the gears were 26 miles per hour in first, 42 miles per hour in second, 68 miles per hour in third, and a theoretical 93.5 miles per hour in fourth. All these speeds are with the standard 4.3:1 rear axle. Optional axle ratios of 3.7:1, 3.9:1, 4.1:1, and 4.55:1 were also available.

Chassis

The MGA was built up from a ladder-type frame, with two parallel box-section side-members and six cross-members. The side and cross-members were spaced far enough apart to allow a low seating position.

Because the MGA as initially conceived was a roadster, the torsional stiffness added by a steel roof was not there. Therefore, a cross-brace was added under the firewall. Tubular cross-members join the two boxed chassis rails at the front, behind the engine, behind the gearbox, in front of the rear axle, and across the rear. Central rigidity was offered by a steel gearbox tunnel that ran the entire length of the cockpit. The floorboards under the pedals and the rear panel were made of plywood. The body was bolted to the chassis at 13 points. Unfortunately, the extra bracing made for a narrow door, which made entry somewhat awkward.

Syd Enever insisted on using 14-gauge steel rather than the standard thinner 16 gauge for the chassis, stating, "You can rust

Even though the MGA 1600 was marketed primarily in the United States, some ads contained both right-hand drive and left-hand drive cars in their illustrations. The reasoning behind this may have been to emphasize the car's British heritage.

away two gauges of metal and still have a motorcar!" This may be the reason for the longevity of the model. Up front was an independent front suspension that was carried over from the Y, MG TD, and MG TF. It incorporated unequal-length wishbones, coil springs, and Armstrong lever-action hydraulic shock absorbers. The suspension was designed by Alec Issigonis and Jack Daniels of Morris. Early in the production run, it was discovered that the springs were too soft and would deteriorate after hard use to a point where the oil pump pickup would be uncovered during hard cornering, resulting in a loss of oil pressure. Stiffer front springs were introduced at chassis No. 15,152. The rear suspension was by semielliptic springs and Armstrong lever-action shocks. The springs were shackled at the rear and controlled by double-piston shocks, which were bolted to the inside of the frame members. While the exterior of the MGA was as modern as any car of its era, the rear suspension was still solid, with a hypoid rear axle.

MGA '1600'

Besides the larger engine that delivered 79.5 brake horsepower versus the 72 of the MGA, the MGA 1600 also had disc brakes for better stopping. Some observers felt the "Safety Fast" slogan meant MGs stopped better than they went. The 1600 was available with disc or wire wheels. Optional extras were a tonneau cover, heater, whitewall tires, and windshield washers.

Brakes

On the MGA 1500, the brakes were the same as the Le Mans cars: 10-inch diameter Lockheed drum brakes on all four wheels with a swept area of 134 square inches. For the higher performance of the MGA Twin Cam, Dunlop-design four-wheel disc brakes were fitted as standard equipment. The MGA 1600 and 1600 Mark II had front disc brakes and rear drum brakes fitted, as was becoming the norm in higher-performance cars of the era. A few 1600s and a few more 1600 Mark IIs were equipped with four-wheel disc brakes.

Body

The MGA body was the last MG to be built using a separate chassis and body design, as the MGB would be a unibody design. The MGA's doors, trunk lid, and hood were aluminum, while the rest of the body was steel. All MGAs were subject to rust, particularly in the area of the rocker panels below the doors. You usually can tell the condition of an MGA simply by checking the rocker panels. If they're in good condition, then it is probable that the rest of the car is in good condition and has been well cared for.

Floors have been known to rot through in well-beaten MGAs, too. However, at this writing it's been 35 years since the last one was built, and if you're buying an A in any kind of decent condition you'll be unlikely to find one with a rotted-through plywood floor. Still, it would be wise to check. The MGA was the first MG sports car to have a trunk. While the carrying capacity wasn't great, there was room for soft-sided luggage around the full-size covered spare. A tool kit was provided, with jack, screwdriver, and pliers, as well as a hammer if the car was equipped with the optional wire wheels or, as in the case of the Twin Cam, center knock-off hubs.

Grilles can be used to differentiate between the 1500/1600/Twin Cam and the 1600 Mark II. All have a rounded, nearly square pattern of 28 vertical chrome slats surrounded by a chrome border. In the 1600

The MGA 1600 was essentially identical physically to the original MGA with few differences. The engine capacity had been increased from 1,489 cc to 1,588 cc and power increased from 68 bhp to 80 bhp. On the outside, the taillights were now dual units and a small "MGA 1600" badge was affixed near the engine exhaust outlets.

Mark II, however, the bottom of the slats was recessed by about 2 inches, making the slats more vertical.

Front parking light lenses changed with each model. On the 1500, they were bullet-shaped and located just below the headlights. On the 1600, the lens was flat, and was a dual function affair. The upper portion was yellow for the turn signal and the lower portion clear as a parking light. A more positive distinction can be made with the taillights. On the 1500, they are simple one-lens lights. On the 1600, the taillight is a dual-lens affair, with a small turn signal lamp mounted above the rear light. On the 1600 Mark II, the lenses are horizontally mounted below the trunk opening, making

for a smoother fender line. A quick-release fuel filler cap is located just above and to the left of the right taillight, on the rear deck on all models.

Coupes

While the roadster was the most popular form of MGA, coupe versions of all four types were available. The coupe was introduced at the London Motor Show in October 1956. In terms of exterior appearance, the coupes resembled roadsters with the optional hardtop fitted. The obvious differences, of course, were in the coupe's wind-up windows and exterior door handles. MGA coupe owners could enter their cars in GT category competition.

The 1600 Mark II had an even larger engine than the 1600, bored out to 1622 cc, increasing power to 95 horsepower at 5,000 rpm. Performance was marginally better than the 1600, but not enough to cause neck-snapping acceleration.

Eric Carter is credited with designing the coupes for Bodies Branch in Coventry, in the experimental department. Progress of the car was hounded over by Eric Carter, Syd Enever, and Jimmy O'Neal. The coupes offered better aerodynamics, which permitted the 1500 to break the 100 mile per hour barrier. The coupes were 65 pounds heavier than the corresponding roadsters, but with better aerodynamics and the four horsepower increase of the engine, announced at the same time, performance did not deteriorate. Initial cost was $245 more than the roadster.

Other amenities offered the coupe owner for his $245 were lockable doors, movable wing windows, inside door pulls, special upholstery on the seats and door panels, map pockets forward of the doors to replace those "lost" from the doors of the roadster, and a small carpeted space behind the seats that was useful for carrying luggage. The instrument panel was covered in vinyl and had chrome trim.

The prime identifying feature of the new 1600 Mark II was the grille, which had slats that were more vertical than on the original MGA grille. The bottoms of the slats were recessed back two inches, giving the car a unique look.

I switched from a used Glacier Blue 1956 MGA 1500 roadster to a Chariot Red 1962 MGA 1600 Mark II coupe when repair costs were too high for the older car. I had owned the 1500 for one year when the master cylinder blew on the way home from work. It was my first week in a new job, and I couldn't afford the $80 repair cost for the cylinder. But I could afford to trade in the older car on the red coupe sitting in the showroom. My soon-to-be wife appreciated the better creature comforts of the closed car.

Tops

Roadster tops were made of a coated fabric with three plastic windows in the back, although some early models had a single rear window. Visibility was decent with the top erected, but no self-respecting sports car owner would have the top up if there was a chance of running with it down. The classic example was to run in the winter with the top down, driver and passenger ensconced in blankets and warm coats, and the heater going full blast. A matching tonneau would protect the seats if you were parking for a while, and you could run the car with the cover over the passenger seat if you were driving solo.

With the top and side curtains down, they stowed neatly in bags behind the seats. The little carrying capacity that existed in that area was reduced to zero with the top dropped. The tops were relatively easy to replace, and replacement was usually necessary if the top had been erected too often. The top on my first MGA had seen better days and I replaced it with one from a wrecked MGA I found in a junkyard. The entire job took less than three hours, with no special tools.

Windows

With the exception of the coupes, MGAs had plastic side curtains. These, too, changed with the change of models, and much better after-market products that improved on the original MG design were available.

On the 1500, the curtains were designed to clip onto the windshield frame, providing support and protection from bowing at top speed.

In time, though, the curtains would bow away from the windshield, creating a gap for cold air and rain. The lower hinged panel of the curtain raised for signalling and toll booths. This section was also lifted to reach inside to pull the string that opened the door, since there were no exterior door handles.

For the 1600, MG introduced sliding plexiglass side curtains, which were a definite improvement over the lifting type of the 1500. They were more rigid and, therefore, offered better protection from the elements.

Wheels

The standard MGA 1500 was fitted with 12-hole disc wheels, while 48-spoke wire wheels were an option and 60-spoke wire wheels were a competition option. This combination continued through the life of the car, except for the Twin Cam, which offered center-lock knock-off disc wheels. One significant MGA was the 1600 Mark II that was the 100,000th MGA. It was built on May 16, 1962, exactly six years after the first MGA 1500 rolled off the line at Abingdon. This car was painted gold, with gold-painted wire wheels, whitewall tires, and a cream interior with white carpeting. It was first displayed at the New York International Automobile Show in 1962.

Restoration and Running

There were 101,081 MGAs of assorted ilk built between September 1955 and June 1962. Therefore, the MGA is not a rare car, and because of these large numbers many are still available. If you're in the market for an MGA in the 1990s, chances are you can find a car in either original or very good shape or one that has been restored at least once. While junkers abound, the majority of MGAs on the road today are either in decent shape or are sturdy enough to have resisted many years of use and are worth restoring. In any case, you'll need to check for rust in the following areas: inside the inner face of the main chassis rails by the seats (if the carpets get wet, they tend to be the source of rust); at the bottom of the A-pillars; between the door sills and the chassis; in the area of the battery boxes (these would corrode on

Taillights on the MGA 1600 Mark II were removed from the fenders, where they had resided since the original MGA, and relocated under the trunk opening. The 1600's two-piece lenses were replaced by one-piece lenses in the Mark II version.

the fenders fit. Also check the straps that hold the fuel tank in place, as these may have rusted through. The cure is to strip the paint off and get down to bare metal, fill any holes with fiberglass or metal filler, apply a good base coat of paint, and build back up from there.

Many poorly restored cars are available. Prospective buyers should check for ill fitting or badly restored bodywork, a flexing chassis, smoking engine, or rough gearbox. Because of the large number of cars built, a good body and chassis are more important than a good engine, because drivetrain components are more readily available than body parts.

The chassis and main body parts are steel, but the doors, hood, and trunk lid are all aluminum. They don't rust. The floor, however, is plywood and is susceptible to rot. The MG Owners' Club has an eight-point checklist for inspecting MGAs for possible restoration projects. Since the MGA

new cars); the cross-members; the trunk floor; the inner fender panel inside the trunk; the corners of the main body section at the lower front; and along the body where

This was the car that continued the love affair for the author. My fiancee, later wife, felt the coupe was more civilized than the roadster because it was more airtight and didn't allow those annoying cold breezes in the face. With continual gaps between the windshield and the plastic side curtains, driving in the winter could be a frigid experience in the convertible.

As with all MGA models, an easy way to determine which engine was under the hood was to look at the air vent. The 1600 Mark II added a plate with that identification next to the engine air vent.

had a separate chassis and body, the restoration project becomes more complex, since it must be assembled accurately to ensure a good final fit.

On initial inspection of the car, you should look for any taper in the gaps between the doors and the body. The fit of the doors is a vital guide to the state of the body tub. Any problem with the fit can only be cured by a total rebuild. Potential buyers are advised to look under the car and examine the gap between the sills and chassis where mud can build up, trap moisture, and cause rust.

The chassis is prone to rust in certain areas, even though it was built of heavy-gauge steel. One such spot is the inside face of the chassis center section, where the floor support rails are attached. Moisture trapped by damp plywood floorboards can corrode the steel box side-members. The chassis may also suffer from stress-induced cracks at the top of the scuttle, surrounding the dash, where it joins the angled front braces.

Replacement body parts are available from several sources, including Moss Motors. They do, however, require skill to fit properly.

Beside the body and frame, the weakest point of the MGA is its independent front suspension. It requires regular lubrication, and any original cars should be checked to see that they are well lubricated. The rack-and-pinion steering is usually trouble free, but should be

checked for tightness. The steering box is also located in front of the car where it is constantly subjected to rocks and mud.

All-drum-brake cars should pose no major problems, but there are problems with cars that have front disc brakes. The chrome-plated calipers may seize, even if the car has only been out of service for a short time. On the Twin Cam, with four-wheel discs, the rears tend to rust badly and the hand brake isn't very efficient. Rear shock absorbers last longer than fronts, but the leaf springs occasionally break.

It is important to check the chassis number and compare it with the original specifications. If the two don't match up, you may be looking at a bastardized restoration (wrong engine, coupe-turned-into roadster, etc.) and your car won't be worth much when you're finished with it. Contact your local MG Car Club for an expert's opinion. MGA engines are known for their sturdiness. Oil pressure should be above 50 psi at 50 miles per hour when the engine is hot. The gearbox is also strong, although synchromesh on second gear may be shot. Oil leaks are common in the B series engine, especially from the rear of the crankshaft. An oily smell from the exhaust is a good indication of wear. Remove the oil filler cap and look for puffs of oily smoke. Also, examine the cylinder head carefully for anti-freeze leaks or stains which can reveal cracks, especially around the spark plugs.

The Twin Cam is another story. The first 345 engines used chrome-plated rings that created excessive bore wear. Prior to engine 1587, the tappet seats were aluminum, as was the head. After that engine, steel sleeves were added that reduced wear. Original Twin Cams used a 9.9:1 compression ratio. This was later reduced to 8.3:1. Most replacement engines have the lower compression ratio. A nonvacuum advance distributor was one of the last modifications made to this engine, and older engines function more efficiently with the vacuum advance disconnected. Oil pressure should be 50 psi at 35 miles per hour in fourth gear.

When changing the fan belt, though, you must remove the radiator. This is to provide

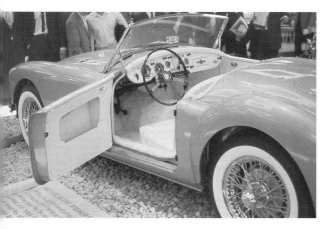

The 100,000th MGA—a significant milestone at the time—was a special gold-painted model with lambswool carpeting that was displayed at the 1962 New York International Auto Show. In reality, the much ballyhooed 100,000th MGA was nearly the last of the model. Only 1,081 more MGAs were built.

This well-restored MGA 1600 Mark II has an after-market wood-rim steering wheel. It is shown with the optional tonneau cover fitted. Tonneau covers allowed the owner/driver to keep the top down and still protect the interior of the car from the sun or occasional rain showers. It was possible to drive an MGA in cold weather with the top down and tonneau fitted, as long as you kept the heater on "high" and dressed warmly.

access to the lower adjusting nut on the generator. Removable panels were fitted inside the wheel arches of later cars. Draining the cooling system requires a separate draining of the block.

Gearboxes can be noisy. Since first gear doesn't have synchromesh, the gear clusters can get damaged and may need to be replaced. The second and third gear synchromesh ring wears out, causing wear on the gear teeth, and the synchro hubs can wear out. Worn gearboxes tend to jump out of third gear. Axles can get noisy but rarely give problems. The 1600 Mark II has a higher rear axle ratio. The Twin Cam gearbox is sturdy, but the rear axle on cars with chassis No. 2371 and above could be a source of trouble. These units had half-shafts that had more splines than the earlier models.

The good news is that parts are readily available, either original or New Old Stock (NOS). Moss Motors Ltd. (see Resource Guide section) is an excellent source of parts for all MGs.

There is always a debate concerning whether one should use original, NOS, or after-market parts. The decision regarding which parts to use for your restoration depends on your goal. If you intend to create a 100-point concours winner, go for original parts in every case. But if your goal is to rebuild the car as accurately as possible for the enjoyment the restoration and eventual driving will give you, then after-market parts are perfectly acceptable.

For example, when I was active in the New Jersey MG Car Club, we had a member who was restoring an MG TC. At that time it was possible to buy original MG parts from J. S. Inskip. But a Ford taillight was so similar to the TC's taillight that the owner decided to use the Ford lens cover rather than the MG. They looked the same, but it wasn't original. This owner's goal was to rebuild the car as a driver and he didn't necessarily care about concours restoration. Unfortunately, the car was destroyed in an accident, so maybe God wasn't in favor of non-MG parts on an MG. The driver survived.

On the other hand, I have a friend who restored a Jaguar 3.8 sedan, and he searched for five years to find a 1/4-inch red reflector to go on the chrome piece on top of the fenders. His goal was for a 100-point restoration.

Essentially undistinguishable from the base MGA, the MGA Twin Cam had a much more powerful engine under the hood. The wheels were different, too. The Twin Cam used center-lock knock-offs, while the standard MGA used four-bolt discs or optional wire wheels.

Once you have your MGA, look after it carefully. In a review of the model in *Thoroughbred & Classic Cars* in January 1995, it was recommended that you clean the underside regularly, especially if you drive the car in areas where the road crews use salt to melt ice and snow. One area deserving special attention is the narrow space between the door sills and the chassis. The magazine also recommended repairing body parts rather than trying to replace them. The simple reason is that on the factory lines, assemblers could choose from long, medium, and short pieces to fit the rest of the body. *Thoroughbred & Classic Cars* also recommends not running radial tires on 48-spoke wire wheels because the wheels aren't strong enough. The alternative is to find 60-spoke wheels from either a used parts supplier or an aftermarket supplier (see Resource Guide section).

Equipped with an after-market luggage rack, the MGA Twin Cam looks like any other MGA. But lurking under the hood was a finicky, double overhead cam four-cylinder engine that, when in proper running order, developed 110 SAE horsepower at 6,750 rpm. This angle also shows the three-window top that most MG owners always found a way to keep stowed behind the front seats in its pouch.

How many are left? *Thoroughbred & Classic Cars* estimated that there were about 1,800 pushrod MGAs in the UK Register and about 3,000 in the United States, but there is some duplication and some cars aren't registered. *T&CC* also estimated that there are 50 Twin Cams in England and maybe 100 in the United States. What are they worth? In a publication such as this, it's impossible to set prices. Do your research before you buy. Don't spend $25,000 for a car that may be worth $15,000. If you don't know what you're looking at, find an expert you can trust from your local MG Car Club. It's worth the price of a couple of beers to get the opinion of someone who knows what he's talking about and knows what to look for.

MGAs on the Road

All MGA gearboxes had synchromesh on the top three gears only, making them difficult to drive in traffic. My only MGA ticket came when I coasted through a stop sign because I was too lazy to come to a complete stop before shifting into first. From a transmission standpoint, all MGAs have similar driving characteristics.

The MGA Twin Cam has the most powerful engine, but like most twin-cam engines of the 1950s, it is temperamental. The problem lies with the cut of the cam and the shapes of the pistons. The tops of the pistons have a wedge shape to increase compression. While the shape served that purpose well, the pistons would hole when they were contacted by the valves, usually on uphill runs.

With a possible 110 horsepower available, compared to the 72 brake horsepower of the original 1500 MGA, the Twin Cam was a potent machine. It was difficult to keep the engine in tune with gasoline that had an octane rating of lower than 100, which was practically all gas at the time. The valves would often meet the pistons if the cams weren' t adjusted properly. Later engines had a lower compression ratio, which lessened the danger of holed pistons.

Flat-topped pistons eliminate the problem, though the compression ratio is reduced.

Below the Twin Cam on the power curve is the MGA 1600 Mark II, with the 1,622-cc engine. This engine develops 90 horsepower, compared to the 68 of the 1500 engine, a 55 percent increase. Consequently, the 1600 Mark II gives more spirited performance.

For overall use, the coupes outshine the roadsters. Early roadsters had flimsy side curtains that were later replaced by sliding plastic side curtains in aluminum frames. These are better, of course, but I've always been spoiled by wind-up windows, so I personally prefer the coupes to the roadsters.

Most people who drive MGAs on a frequent basis, however, drive the roadsters.

There is always a special thrill to driving an open sports car. Most MG driving in the United States these days is on "special" days, either to meets or when nice weather permits top-down motoring. In this case, the roadster is definitely the choice, because in warmer weather the coupes are confining and stuffy, as air conditioning was not an option.

Modern driving of an MGA can be hazardous, however. Wade Cruse, who owns an MGA 1500 that he drives frequently, said the biggest hazard is with drivers who will come right up on his rear bumper trying to identify the car. "It's worst at night," he said, "because their headlights are higher than my car and they shine right in the rearview mirror."

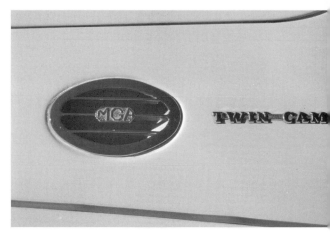

Like the 1600 and 1600 Mark II, the MGA Twin Cam can be identified by a chrome label next to the engine hot air vent.

Many a modern door handle designer could take a cue from the MGA coupe's design, which was simple and effective. Those of us who moved from roadsters to coupes were constantly banging our knuckles on the windows as we tried to reach through them to open the doors from the inside.

The Achilles heel of the MGA Twin Cam might well have been the suspension, which was the same as that used with the standard MGA. The car had four-wheel disc brakes and knock-off wheels, but the suspension, while good enough for the standard MGAs, could have used some improvement in the hotter Twin Cam. Competition parts were available, and wise owners fitted them.

By far the most civilized MGA was the Sports Coupe, fixed head coupe, or simply, coupe. Everything under the skin was identical to the then-current MGA roadster, but the coupe offered wind-up windows, exterior door handles, and a lockable driver's door that provided more security.

There was even a small cargo area behind the seats that was large enough for a briefcase or book bag. Visibility was also better with the coupe, as the wraparound rear window gave a better view of what was behind than did the three-window soft top.

SPECIFICATIONS

MGA1500

Production dates: Roadster—9/55–5/59; Coupe—12/56–5/59
Total production: 58,750 (52,478 Roadsters, 6,272 Coupes)
Chassis numbers: HD 10,101-68,850
Engine numbers: 15GB, 15GD
Price: Roadster—$2,195; Coupe—$2,750
Engine:

> Type: Cast iron inline four cylinder
> Displacement: 1,489 cc
> Bore: 73.025 mm
> Stroke: 89.0 mm
> Compression ratio: 8.3:1
> BHP: 68 @ 5,500 rpm (later 72 @ 5,750 rpm)
> Torque: 77.4 ft-lbs @ 3,500 rpm (later 80.2 ft-lbs @ 3,850 rpm)
> Red line: 5,800 rpm

Transmission:

> Type: Four-speed with synchromesh on top three gears
> Clutch: 8-in single dry plate
> Overall gear ratios:
>> 4th*   1.00:1
>> 3rd*   1.374:1
>> 2nd*   2.214:1
>> 1st   3.64:1
>> Reverse 4.76:1
>> *Synchromesh
> Rear axle ratio: Standard 4.3:1, optional 3.7, 3.9, 4.1, 4.55:1

Chassis:

> Type: Box-section steel with tubular cross members
> Wheels and tires: Perforated steel disc wheels standard, 48-spoke wire wheels optional, alloy rim 60-spoke wire wheels competition option
> Tire size: 5.50x15 with disc wheels; 5.60x15 with wire wheels
> Brakes: Lockheed hydraulic with 10-in drums, two leading shoes at front
> Steering: Rack and pinion
> Front suspension: Independent by coil springs and wishbone, Armstrong lever-action hydraulic shock absorbers
> Rear suspension: Nonindependent by semielliptic leaf springs, Armstrong hydraulic lever-action shock absorbers
> Electrical: 12-volt positive ground, 51 ampere-hour battery (two 6-volt batteries in series)

Fuel system:

Fuel tank: 12-gallon tank with single high-pressure SU electric fuel pump
Dimensions:

> Wheelbase: 94.0 in
> Overall length: 156.0 in
> Track front: 47.5 in (disc wheels); 47.875 in (wire wheels)
> Track rear: 48.75 in

Width: 58.0 in
Height: 50.0 in
Ground clearance: 6.0 in
Curb weight: 1,988 lbs (Roadster); 2,107 lbs (Coupe)
Colors:

Exterior: Black (red or green seats, Ice Blue top), Orient Red (red or black seats, black top), Tyrolite Green (gray or black seats, Ice Blue top), green, Ash Green (gray or black seats, Ice Blue top), Glacier Blue (gray or black seats, Ice Blue top), Old English White (red or black seats, black top), Mineral Blue (Coupe only with gray seats)
Tops: Black and Ice Blue
Interior: Black, red, green, gray
Significant chassis modifications:

Chassis number 10917 (disc wheels) or 11450 (wire wheels) onward: Modified rear axle hub bearing nuts
Chassis number 15152 onward: Modified front coil springs
Chassis number 16101 onward: New top introduced with seams stitched, lapped and welded
Chassis number 24954 onward: Additional accelerator return spring added
Chassis number 61504 (15GD engines) onward: New engine, designated 15GD, fitted
Driver's Handbook factory part number: AKD598G
Workshop Manual factory part number: AKD600C
Parts List factory part number: AKD1055
Special Tuning Manual factory part number: AKD819D

MGA Twin Cam
Production dates: 9/58–6/60
Total production: 1,788 Roadsters; 323 Coupes
Chassis numbers: YD1-501–YD1-2611
Base price: Roadster—$3,345; Coupe—$3,550
Engine:

Type: Cast iron double overhead cam inline four cylinder
Displacement: 1,588 cc
Bore: 75.4 mm
Stroke: 88.9 mm
Compression ratio: 9.9:1 (8.3:1)
BHP: 108 (net) @ 6,700 rpm; 110 (max SAE) @ 6,750 rpm; 100 (net w/8.3:1 pistons) @ 6,700 rpm
Torque: 105 ft-lbs @ 4,500 rpm
Red line: 7,000 rpm
Transmission: Same as MGA 1500
Chassis: Same as MGA 1500 except:

Wheels and tires: Dunlop center-lock steel disc wheels with Dunlop 5.90x15 Road Speed tires
Brakes: Lockheed discs front and rear
Dimensions: Same as MGA 1500 except:

Curb weight: 2,185 lbs (Roadster); 2,222 lbs (Coupe)
Colors: Same as MGA 1500
Significant production modifications:

Chassis number 528 onward: Modified engine mounting and air cleaner

Chassis number 2192 (Coupe) and 2193 (Roadster) onward: Bodies modified to include tail light plinths and front flashing indicator mountings

Chassis number 2275 onward: Anti-roll bar assembly introduced

Chassis number 2371 onward: Modified halfshafts; later models, modified wheel arches including louvered detachable panels in the front wheel arches

Driver's Handbook factory part number: AKD879A. After car number 2193, part number AKD979B applies; also free supplement AKD1412

Workshop Manual factory part number: AKD926A

Parts List factory part number: AKD1296

MGA 1600

Production dates: 5/59–4/61

Total production: 28,730 Roadsters, 2,771 Coupes

Chassis numbers: G/HN 68851–100351

Engine numbers: 16GA

Base price: Roadster—$2,485; Coupe—$2,706

Engine:

> Type: Cast iron inline four cylinder
> Displacement: 1,588 cc
> Bore: 75.4 mm
> Stroke: 88.9 mm
> Compression ratio: 8.3:1
> BHP: 78 @ 5,500 rpm
> Torque: 87 ft-lbs @ 3,800 rpm
> Red line: 5,800 rpm

Transmission/rear axle: Same as MGA 1500

Chassis: Same as MGA 1500 except:

> Weight: 2,016 lbs
> Brakes: Lockheed discs front, drums rear
> Colors:
>> Exterior: Alamo Beige (red seats, beige top), Chariot Red (red or beige seats, beige top), Iris Blue (black seats, blue top), Dove Gray (red seats, gray top), Old English White (red or black seats, gray top), black (beige or red seats, gray top)
>> Tops: Beige, gray, blue
>> Interiors: Red, beige, black
> Significant production modifications:
>> Chassis number 68851 onward: Aluminum deluxe sliding side screens available as an option
>> Chassis number 70222 onward: Sealed beam headlamps fitted to cars exported to the U.S.

Driver's Handbook factory part number: AKD1172B

Workshop Manual factory part number: AKD600C

Parts List factory part number: AKD1215

Special Tuning Manual factory part number: AKD819D

MGA 1600 Mk II

Production dates: 4/61–6/62

Total production: 8,198 Roadsters, 521 Coupes

Chassis numbers: G/HN2 100352-109070

Engine numbers: 16GC

Base price: Roadster—$2,485; Coupe—$2,706

Engine:

> Type: Cast iron inline four cylinder
>
> Displacement: 1,622 cc
>
> Bore: 76.2 mm
>
> Stroke: 89 mm
>
> Compression ratio: 8.9:1
>
> BHP: 90 @ 5,500 rpm
>
> Torque: 97 ft-lbs @ 4,000 rpm

Transmission: Same as MGA 1500 except:

> Overall gear ratios:
>
>> 4th*   1.00:1
>>
>> 3rd*   1.374:1
>>
>> 2nd*   2.214:1
>>
>> 1st   3.64:1
>>
>> Reverse 4.76:1
>>
>> *Synchromesh
>
> Rear axle ratio: 4.1:1

Chassis: Same as MGA 1500

> Brakes: Lockheed discs front, drums rear
>
> Colors:
>
>> Exterior: Chariot Red (red or beige seats, beige top), Iris Blue (black seats, blue top), Alamo Beige (red seats, beige top), Dove Gray red seats, gray top), Old English White (red or black seats, gray top), black (beige or red seats, gray top)
>>
>> Tops: Beige, blue, gray
>>
>> Interior: Red, Beige, Black
>
> Significant production modifications:
>
>> Chassis 100352 onward: Anchorage points for seat belt mountings for driver and passenger incorporated into chassis
>>
>> Chassis numbers 102589 (disc wheels) and 102929 (wire wheels): Disc brake dust covers installed to reduce wear
>>
>> Chassis number 102737 onward: Oil cooler kits fitted to all export cars
>>
>> Chassis number 103261 (disc wheels) and 103834 (wire wheels) onward: Modified disc brake caliper dust shield introduced
>>
>> Chassis number 103857 onward: Mk X sealed beam headlight units fitted to all cars exported to the U.S.

Driver's Handbook factory part number: AKD1958B

Workshop Manual factory part number: AKD600C

Parts List factory part number: AKD1215

Special Tuning Manual factory part number: AKD819D

Chapter 4

MGB

★★★★★	MGC
★★★★★	MGB
★★★★	MGB V-8
★★★✦	MGB Mark II
★★★	MGC/GT
★★★	MGB/GT
★★	MGB (black bumper)
★★	MGB/GT Mark II

Shortly after the completion of EX181, the MGA-based land speed record setter, John Thornley, the General Manager of MG, began thinking about the car that would replace it. EX181 had set five new Class F speed records at the Bonneville Salt Flats, with Stirling Moss driving. First, with a 1,489-cc supercharged Twin-Cam engine, Moss drove at 245.64 miles per hour in August 1957. In September 1959, Phil Hill took the same car and reached 254.91 miles per hour over the flying kilometer.

Thornley's inspiration for a new MG design came from, of all marques, Aston Martin. "My imagination was fired by seeing a trio of Aston Martin DB2/4 coupes competing in a production car race at Silverstone," he wrote in his autobiography. "I can remember seeing the three of them, side by side, on the track, to this day. I thought, 'That's the shape our new car ought to be.' "

The first leanings toward a new design (and designation) came in 1957, when a new experimental number, EX205, was issued for an "MG 2-seater (MGB)." The first design penned under EX205 by chief body engineer Jim O'Neill was called "a very fat, sexy looking lady." It was called 205/1.

Frua was given an opportunity to design a possible MGA replacement, and it earned designation EX205/2R. The car had a Maserati-like front end and an MGB-like rear, but it was felt that it looked heavy. Also, Frua painted it Ferrari red, which wasn't diplomatically

The original 1962 MGB was a simple car, much like the MGA. While it could be ordered with wire wheels that would soon go out of style (and tune), the MGB also had a relatively simple engine that was easy to work on and delivered reasonably good performance.

correct. To escape paying import duties, BMC brought the car into the country as a design exercise, and it had to be either exported or destroyed. It was destroyed, although dimensions were taken on the car.

In 1958, a new designer was on the scene, Don Hayter. Hayter had been involved in the design of the MGA coupe. He also had worked with Frank Feeley, who was responsible for the design of the Aston Martin DB2/4 that had inspired John Thornley. Hayter first designed a roadster in 1958 on an MGA chassis. Examination of the model shows the car has lines that evolved into the final MGB, although it still had an MGA-type grille. A full-sized closed coupe was built off this design and it was very Aston-like, with true fastback styling and the mock MGA grille. Most of the features of this car were then transferred to another Hayter design, EX214/1, which was essentially the MGB in its final form. Hayter's pencil drawing of EX214/1 is dated June 19, 1958.

A prototype was built from this design that included a 1,588-cc MGA engine and coil spring rear axle. Neither the engine nor the coil spring suspension would survive to production. Three prototypes were eventually built before a batch of eight preproduction cars went down the line at Abingdon. In its final form the "B" showed some differences from the prototypes: 14-inch wheels as opposed to the 15-inch wheels of the MGA, and a 1,798-cc inline four instead of the originally proposed 1,622-cc unit from the MGA 1600 Mark II. The Mark II engine was the first choice, but the MGB ended up at about 100 pounds heavier, which cut top speed from 100 miles per hour in the MGA to around 94 in the "B." This was unacceptable, so the engine was bored out to 1,798 cc by increasing the bore from 76.2 to 80.3 mm.

Production

The first MGB was built in May 1962 and proved to be an instant success. Here, at last, was a true MG convertible, with roll-up windows and lockable doors and trunk. In its initial form, the MGB was 2 inches wider than the MGA and about 3 inches shorter. Monocoque construction permitted the

MG took full advantage of the homonymy between the new model name and the buzzy insect with this ad which crowed about the new car's advantages over the unmentioned MGA, including a larger, more powerful engine, wind-up windows, and a larger trunk.

designers to move the firewall and pedals forward by 6 inches, which created more legroom, although it also meant the passengers were sitting closer to the engine. In addition, this extra space meant that there could be a decent rear seat in the "B" as well as a trunk that held more than a spare tire. According to one source, John Thornley was able to get his four grandchildren into the back seat of his MGB.

With monocoque construction, the MGB's chassis was extremely strong. The platform was reinforced on each side by a box-section member. Individual chassis members swept up over the rear axle and provided mounting points for the rear suspension. Up front, the engine was mounted on two box-section pieces that ran forward

The original MGB also abandoned the vertical chrome slats of the T-series and MGA grilles. Instead, it had a chrome bezel around a mesh grille.

from a cross-member located below the front seats. This "double bulkhead" offered extreme rigidity. Any front suspension loads were transferred to the double bulkhead through the longitudinal engine members and the inner fender panels. The firewall was attached to the transmission tunnel by a box-section piece. Chassis stiffness was improved by a square section support for the bulkhead from the gearbox cover, which also contained a radio speaker.

With a side profile that no longer featured the familiar flowing lines of the MGA, the MGB was an obvious change. The car had wind-up windows for the first time (not counting the MGA coupes) and smaller diameter wheels that gave it a more aerodynamic look.

The MGB's suspension was similar to that of the MGA, with detail differences. Among those detail differences were 73 pound/inch front coil springs, as opposed to the 100 pound/inch springs of the MGA. At the rear, the spring leaves were lengthened by 2 inches. In addition, a seventh leaf was added. Softer settings were used on the lever arm rear shocks than those used on the MGA, all of which led to a softer ride for the "B" over the "A."

The MGB's 14-inch wheels (as opposed to the 15-inch wheels on the MGA) produced a change in the rear axle ratio from 4.1:1 to 3.9:1. Standard wheels were four-bolt discs with 4J rims and 5.60x14 Dunlop tires. Smaller tires meant smaller Lockheed front disc brakes; 10.75-inch diameter discs were used versus 11-inch discs in the MGA. The rear drum brakes were unchanged.

The engine was physically similar to the MGA's, but had the extra 4-mm bore to increase capacity to 1,798 cc and brake horsepower to 95 at 5,400 rpm. In addition, the three-bearing crankshaft was strengthened, with 2.125-inch bearings instead of the 2-inch bearings on the A. Cylinder heads of the B and A were almost identical, but the compression ratio of the B was reduced from 9.0:1 to 8.8:1. Carburetion was through twin 1-inch SU HS4 carburetors, which used Cooper paper air cleaners that had a different look than those of the MGA.

MG offered a Laycock de Normanville overdrive unit for the MGB beginning in 1963. The unit was a smaller version of the one used on the Austin-Healey 3000, and was engaged by means of a toggle switch on the dash. The switch was located on left-hand-drive cars next to the fuel gauge. Overdrive could be engaged on third and fourth gears.

At the time of the MGB's construction, Abingdon was only an assembly facility. All the car's parts were shipped from remote locations. The bodies, for example, were built at the Pressed Steel Company near Swindon and were trucked to the BMC Morris Bodies Branch in Coventry, where they were painted. The bodies were then trucked, six at a time, to Abingdon. The dash panel, instruments, seats, and carpeting were

The MGB had considerably more interior room than its predecessor. Driver and passenger had more hip- and leg-room, while there was a small amount of luggage space behind the seats. The B's trunk was also larger than that of the A, which made the after-market luggage rack on this car somewhat redundant.

added on the top floor. Then the chassis were lowered to the next level where they received suspensions, rear axles, and steering gear.

Next came the installation of the engine and gearbox. These parts came from BMC's Longbridge factory. Dunlop wheels and tires were installed last. After assembly, the cars received a 12-mile road test, to Marcham village and back. If they passed the test, they were returned to the factory for shipping. MG built 23,308 MGB roadsters in 1963, its

As with the car, the MGB's engine was all new. With a capacity of 1,788 cc delivering 102 horsepower, the four-cylinder was an improvement over the 1.6-liter in the MGA. Still, it was attached to a four-speed manual transmission with synchromesh only on the top three gears.

first year of production. The following year saw production increase to 26,542. For 1965, the engine received a new five-bearing bottom end. This design was borrowed from the Austin 1800 engine, which had the same 1,798-cc capacity.

A factory hardtop was available for the MGB, but it became somewhat redundant when the MGB/GT was introduced.

MGB/GT

Once the MGB had established itself on the markets, John Thornley returned to the concept of a true GT car. "I wanted to produce a car that no managing director would be ashamed to leave in his car park," he wrote in his autobiography.

Design number EX227 was taken out for a conversion that was penned by MG design employee Jim Stimson. The quarter-scale model was, according to Don Hayter, a lot like the Aston Martin that had inspired Thornley earlier. MG also asked Pininfarina to build a coupe. The eventual car Pininfarina delivered to MG "was really super," according to Hayter. One difference between MG's design exercise and the Pininfarina coupe was a windshield that was 2 inches taller. In addition, Pininfarina had added feature lines that lent a sharpness to the overall appearance. Pininfarina also delivered full-size body sections on Mylar film that Pressed Steel was able to turn into production drawings. The Pininfarina design was chosen because, as Jonathan Wood and Lionel Burrell wrote in MGB: *The Illustrated History*, "The Italian styling house had increased the height of the windscreen by 2 inches over the roadster and the Turin maestros also contributed feature lines which added an extra crispness to the car's appearance."

The coupe was announced at the 1965 London Motor Show. *Autocar* said it was

The MGB's instrument panel offered the driver all the necessary information. A tachometer and speedometer dominated the view immediately in front of the driver, while the fuel level and oil pressure gauges were to the left, and an analog clock and coolant temperature gauges were mounted to the right.

Every MG from the A to the B used "lift the dot" fasteners to attach the top and/or tonneau cover to the body.

"one of the prettiest sports coupes ever to leave the BMC drawing boards." The MGB/GT was almost identical mechanically to the roadster with a few exceptions because of the increased weight. For example, the GT had a standard front sway bar, which was optional on the roadster. The rear springs were upgraded as well to compensate for the extra weight, but since this tended to induce oversteer, the front sway bar was needed. In addition, the front springs were upgraded to 100-pound units from 90-pound units. The GT also used a Salisbury-type rear axle, which was produced by BMC's Tractors and Transmissions Division. The roadster used the same banjo-type rear axle that was used on the MGA, but it caused noise problems. The Salisbury unit avoided much of the banjo unit's self-generated noise. This style unit was added to the roadster in 1967.

BMC said the GT was not just a hardtop version of the MGB, it was an entirely new body style—albeit based on the highly successful and established line of the MGB. The windshield was 4 inches taller, and the wind-up windows were 1 inch taller to produce more glass area. Rearward vision was also improved with the large rear hatch window and two rear quarter windows, hinged at the forward edges. The rear hatch had concealed hinges and spring-loaded supports to make lifting it a one-hand effort.

One feature that remained in the original GT was dual 6-volt batteries, which would stay with the car until 1975. A heater was standard equipment on the GT, but would remain an option on the roadster until 1969. The 1965 MGB/GT weighed 2,379 pounds, or 251 pounds more than the roadster's 2,128 pounds. *Motor* road-tested the GT in February 1966 and achieved a 0-60 miles per hour time of 13.2 seconds, compared to 12.6 seconds for the roadster. Top speed of the GT was 103.3 miles per hour, though, because of lower drag than with the roadster, which recorded a top of 102.8 miles per hour.

With extensive additional sound deadening materials and improved aerodynamics, the MGB/GT was the quietest MG ever built. One obvious advantage of the GT over the roadster was its usable rear seat. While it certainly wasn't large enough to accommodate adults, small children could ride back there in some comfort. The seats would fold flat, creating a nice-sized luggage compartment.

MGB Mark II

The Mark II version of the MGB was introduced in October 1967 as a 1968 model.

The interior of the MGB was thoroughly modern, at least for the era. It had a center console over the transmission tunnel that served as armrest and storage area. Features such as the locking glovebox were not often found in sports cars.

Prime among the new features was an all-synchromesh gearbox, something that MGs had suffered without for many years; the Triumph TR series had used all-synchromesh gearboxes since 1962. The all-synchromesh gearbox could be identified from inside the car by a round gear shift knob, which replaced the egg-shaped knob of the older box. An automatic transmission also became available, which necessitated enlarging the transmission tunnel and, of course, insulted the purists. Only about 5,000 MGBs were equipped with automatic transmissions until the option was discontinued in 1973.

For the 1968/69 model years, the power dropped, thanks to the installation of emissions controls on the engines. An alternator and negative ground was introduced on the Mark II in place of the generator and positive ground that had been used on earlier MGs. A pre-engaged starter also replaced the Bendix type.

For safety, U.S.-spec cars had dual circuit brakes and energy absorbing steering columns. Models sold in the United States after the beginning of 1968 also had three windshield wipers. A year later, fender mounted reflectors, later replaced by side warning lights, were fitted.

U.S.-spec engines were also modified to cope with increased attention to emissions. An engine-driven injection pump was added to force air into the exhaust ports so that unburned gases would finish combusting. In addition, there was a relief valve to limit the pump's output at high engine speeds, and a nonreturn valve to prevent blow-back.

Nineteen sixty-eight MGBs also had a special dash, which had a recessed instrument panel. On the passenger side, the glovebox was removed and replaced with a deeply padded dash, covered in black leather cloth, that was referred to as the "Abingdon Pillow."

The MGB/GT closely approximated what John Thornley was thinking of when he first proposed the "B." Its design is similar to a pair of racing Aston Martins that Thornley had seen.

The glovebox would return in 1972. All the instruments were still there, but they were smaller, and with nonreflective rims. Toggle switches were outlawed by U.S. regulations, and MG didn't think the acceptable rocker switches would do the job, so they were replaced by two multipurpose stalks mounted on the steering column. These stalks controlled turn indicators, horn, headlight dipping and flashing, two-speed wipers, electric windshield washers, and overdrive. Still on the dash were the controls for the heater/defroster, main lighting, and heater fan and choke. The ignition/starter key-switch was also mounted on the steering column.

MGB Fifth Series

Introduced in October 1969 as a 1970 model. This was, actually, the fourth series MGB, since engine and other modifications to earlier Series I cars were not granted new Mark status. More than 20 styling changes were announced. Major among these was the switch to a recessed blacked-out grille inside a thin bright surround molding with an MG octagon in the center. Models headed for the United States had side marker lights at the leading edge of the front fenders. By 1971, rubber-tipped bumper guards were added, leading to the eventual destruction of front-end styling of the car. A trunk light was a handy improvement. MG's membership in the British Leyland Motor Corporation was indicated by small Leyland badges on the front fenders.

Mag-style Rubery Owen steel Rostyle wheels were standard. Radial tires (155x14 on the roadster, 165x14 on the MGB/GT) were standard. Styling changes inside showed a move toward economy. Vinyl upholstery replaced leather, while a smaller leather-covered steering wheel was standard. Other standard equipment included reclining Ambla vinyl bucket seats with

With the rear hatch open, the MGB revealed a decently sized trunk for a small car. In addition, the floor of the trunk was flat and carpeted, something one didn' t always find in either sedans or sports cars.

adjustable headrests, padded sun visors, three-point seatbelts, a heater/defroster, front and rear lighted side markers, lighter and ashtray, map pocket, fitted carpeting, rubber floor mats, and sill kick plates.

The GT coupe continued with space in the rear for additional seating that folded flat for extra storage. Both models had roll-up windows and hinged vent windows. For the 1971 model year, both the MGB and MGB/GT received another grille restyling, in blacked-out form again. Steering column locks became standard in the 1971 model year. In May 1971, MG built its 250,000th MGB, a U.S.-spec MGB/GT. Standard colors in 1970 were Flame Red, Bronze Yellow, British Racing Green, Blue Royale, Pale Primrose, and Glacier White.

MGB Mark III

Introduced October 1971 as a 1972 model. Among the changes were a new center console and armrests. The restyled instrument panel and dash included a lockable glovebox. The place that formerly housed the radio now held a pair of swiveling fresh air ducts. The radio was moved to the console below the dash. In another safety move, rocker switches replaced toggle switches.

The engine was modified for use with low-lead or regular fuel. Capacity was still 1,978 cc, but the compression ratio was reduced to 8.0:1 and brake horsepower fell to 78.5 at 5,500 rpm. Torque was 94 foot-pounds at 3,000 rpm. Seats in the MGB/GT had leather inserts. Three body colors were added: gold, aqua, and dark green. For the 1973 model year, the grille was revised again, this time with the octagon emblem returned to the upper grille molding. The grille itself was black mesh with a chrome surround. Windshield wipers were matte black-finished rather than chrome. For 1974, the last year of production for the Mark III version, the front bumper guards were much thicker, which added to the car's overall length.

MGB Mark IV

The most significant styling change for the Mark IV MGB was large matte black polyurethane nose and tail sections for the 1975 model year. For the remainder of the MGB's life, no chrome bumpers or grille would be seen. The MGB/GT was dropped. The new grille added 70 pounds to the overall weight and five inches to its length. Ride height also went up 1 inch by packing the front suspension. The rear springs were also raised to increase ride height, which tended to mess up the car's handling.

Jim O'Neill, who designed the rubber bumpers for MG, said the job was the most difficult in his life. He is quoted by David Knowles in *MG V-8: Twenty-one Years on . . . From Introduction to RV-8*, "The regulations called for a vehicle to be able to sustain an impact of 5 miles per hour with no damage whatsoever—hydraulics, leaf springs, and canvas-reinforced rubber were all tried, but all proved unacceptable. It soon became apparent that a polyurethane bumper, constructed in such a way as to absorb an impact progressively, was our only hope; and even this was proving difficult at the stipulated -40 degrees. I visited the authorities in

The MGB/GT was a classic grand tourer, with seating for two passengers in comfort and another two in discomfort. Under the rear hatch, there was enough carrying capacity for a decent amount of luggage.

Hatchbacks were the styling excess of the 1960s, and the MGB/GT was MG's answer to the fad. The rear hatch of the GT lifted to expose a flat carpeted floor that was useful as a good-sized trunk, unlike previous MGs. There were small seats behind the two buckets up front, but they were best used in the collapsed position, which increased trunk space.

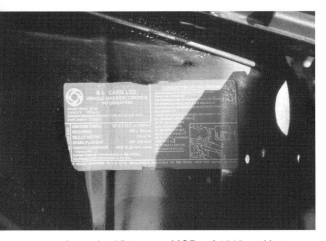

A required fixture on MGBs of 1968 and later was the U.S. Federal Emissions sticker, certifying that the vehicle met the government's requirements for reduced pollutants.

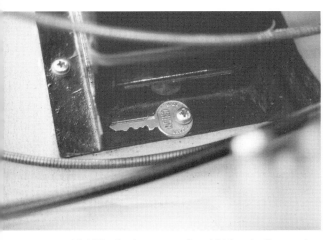

All MGs had a spare key hidden in the engine compartment, attached by a Phillips screw.

Washington for a clarification or easing of their requirements but to no avail.

"To conform with the regulations, we needed a bumper depth of 6 inches. Imagine what this looked like when applied to a small car! By styling the bumper material up and around the grille, a more acceptable shape was arrived at, disguising the massive steel armature beneath."

Engine modifications included a switch from twin SU carburetors to a single Zenith-Stromberg unit. This switch caused a drop in

brake horsepower to 62.5 at 5,500 rpm and a drop in torque to 86 foot-pounds at 2,500 rpm. Actually, the engine was no longer the "B" series engine that had powered MGBs since the beginning, but a new "O" series mill. To improve fuel economy, transmission gear ratios were changed. In 1975, 750 special edition "Jubilee" GT models were built to celebrate MG's 50th anniversary. These cars were painted British Racing Green with gold side stripes, tinted glass, headrests, overdrive, and V-8-style wheels. Decals on the sides of the car read "MG 1925-1975."

MGC-MGC/GT

The MGC, introduced at the 1967 Motor Show as a 1968 model, was originally called the "MG Series MGC," a confusing name that was immediately shortened. The MGC used a 2.9-liter six-cylinder engine with internal dimensions identical to those of the Austin-Healey 3000 six. It was, however, a completely new engine, with seven main bearings, compared to four mains on the older Healey engine. BMC planners, contemplating an eventual replacement for the Austin-Healey 3000, had begun discussing a six-cylinder MGB as early as January 1961. The new engine was smaller in external size than the Healey unit, which made it attractive for the MG, although it weighed 567 pounds, 199 pounds more than the MGB four-cylinder.

Actually, what became the MGC was supposed to have a twin, the Austin-Healey Mark IV. Donald and Geoff Healey were supportive of the joint venture, primarily because of the economics involved. The original engine for the joint venture was to be a 2,660-cc four, but it wouldn't fit in the MGB's engine bay. A lighter version of the Healey six was used instead.

The Healey version of the car was essentially identical to the MGC, but with a Healey grille designed by Don Hayter, bumper overriders, and a few detail changes. The Healeys felt that the changes were less than ideal; in fact, they hated the car's handling and the engine. The problem was that the Morris six was a sedan engine and was too sluggish for a sports car. The

Healeys dropped out of the discussions at a late stage, but with very little loss of money to BMC because the changes to turn the "C" into a Healey would have been minor.

The main distinguishing features between the MGC and the MGB are two bulges in the hood to accommodate the larger radiator and frontmost carburetor. The MGC also used 15-inch wheels, rather than the 14-inch wheels of the MGB. With the power bulge and taller, wider tires, the MGC looked chunkier than the MGB, although the dimensions were essentially identical.

An all-new fully synchronized gearbox became available with the "C." This, combined with the optional automatic transmission, meant that the gearbox tunnel had to be widened. A Laycock overdrive was an optional extra with the manual gearbox. A new exhaust system was partly recessed under the body to the left of the gearbox. The fully synchronized gearbox and overdrive also became available on the "B," as did the automatic transmission.

The Borg-Warner automatic transmission that became available also required significant structural redesign at the front of the car. The gear quadrant was P, R, N, D, L2, L1 for the automatic. The reason for the changes was that the new engine's length was such that the standard MGB suspension's cross-member could not be used. A new cross-member was designed that mirrored the contours of the oil sump and swept up the sides of the engine to be incorporated into new inner fender linings. This also meant that the front suspension had to be completely redesigned. This design included a widely spaced upper wishbone, while the lower member was a single link made up of two channel sections forgings bolted back-to-back, connected to an adjustable torsion bar that ran halfway down the side of the car. Telescopic shock absorbers replaced the lever type of the MGB.

For safety, there were "anti-burst door locks" with flush-fitting interior handles. Owner maintenance became easier with the "C," with a readily accessible distributor mounted high, and the oil dipstick located at the front of the engine. The oil filter was also

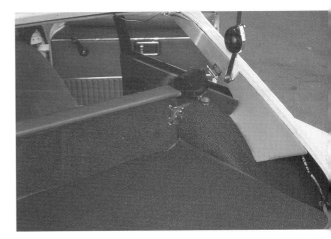

The MGB/GT's rear hatch was kept open with a strut. The floor of the trunk was well-finished with carpeting, and utilized a fold-down panel that also served as the squab for the rear seats.

Concessions to modernity on the MGB/GT included a locking fuel filler cap and back-up light next to the multifunction taillight.

mounted up high on the side where it would be easy to change when necessary, and all the spark plugs were within easy reach.

Performance of the MGC was an improvement over the MGB, with a top speed in the neighborhood of 120 miles per hour, about 20 miles per hour faster than the "B." Compared with the Austin-Healey 3000, though, which used a similar powerplant, the figures were closer. According to *Autocar*, the Healey had a top speed of 121 miles per hour and would go from 0 to 60 miles per hour in 9.8 seconds. The "C" did the 0-60 run in 10 seconds and had a top speed of 120 miles per hour. The Healey weighed 127 pounds more than the "C" but returned 20.3 miles per gallon to the MG's 17.5 miles per gallon. The cars were similarly priced as well, with the MGC being £25 less than the Healey, about $50 in that era.

Complaints about the MGC were primarily that it would go well in a straight line but wouldn't handle the corners that well. To quote *Classic & Sportscar*, "In an effort to help turn the wheels, BMC lowered the steering ratio, meaning more twiddles for the same amount of corner, and decreased the castor, both of which have the effect of deadening the steering. Coupled with inadequate runner, this made the understeer police cry foul at the car's launch in 1967." But the magazine also said, "The C is the car the B should

Both wire wheels and mag-style "Rostyle" wheels were available on the MGB. The era of wire wheels was fast ending, though, and most owners chose the easier-to-maintain Rostyle wheels.

You could conceivably drive or ride in an MGB/GT "dressed to the nines," where such an outfit would have been impractical in an MGA. The MGB was a far more civilized car than its predecessor.

have been," because of its ability to cover ground without tiring the driver and the comfort of the ride. The advantage of the restored 1990s MGC the magazine tested in 1997 was its better rubber, 185/70R15 radials, that changed the character.

MGB/V-8

In 1970, U.K. MG converter Ken Costello had begun installing 3.5-liter Rover V-8 engines in MGB chassis. Costello eventually converted more than 200 MGBs to V-8 specifications. The classic Costello V-8 also has a unique grille, with a black egg-crate design and no MG badging. MG liked the conversion and decided to make its own Rover-powered MG. The first conversion took 28 days from inception, and used a hood with a bulge, similar to the Costello conversion and the MGC, to clear the SU carburetors. The decision was made to go ahead with a production conversion.

MG and Rover both belonged to British Leyland at the time (in the mid-1990s, the MG name and production was held by Rover, which is now owned by BMW). Therefore, a supply of the 3,528-cc Rover engines was at hand. These engines were originally designed by General Motors for use in the Buick Special and Oldsmobile F85 of 1961 and 1962. When Rover felt it needed a better engine than that used in the P2000 (a 2-liter four), it first considered a six. But J. Bruce McWilliams, then president of Rover's North American operations, suggested using a small American V-8 engine. Discussions ensued, and the 215-cubic-inch all-aluminum engine was modified for use in the Rover.

A few modifications were required for the final installation. First, the carburetors were relocated closer to the firewall, eliminating the need for a bulge in the hood. Modifications to the inlet manifold were required. A new alternator was added, and the oil filter was located in series with the oil cooler, because its original location would have interfered with the sway bar. Twin electric fans were located in front of the radiator, a change that was also made to the MGB later. The conversion was made to the MGB/GT chassis because it had greater torsional stiffness than the roadster. Other modifications to the chassis included reshaping the inner fender wells to comply with the wider engine, and chassis members supporting the engine were strengthened. The firewall was slightly altered and the radiator enlarged. The engine's compression ratio was 8.25:1, rather than the 10.5:1 used in the Rover 3500. The exhaust manifolds were also redesigned. It was rated at 137 horsepower at 5,000 rpm.

Externally, there was a modest "V-8" badge added to the grille and tail. Larger wheels and tires were used: 175x14 in the V-8 compared to 165x14 in the standard GT. The wheels combined a machined cast aluminum center riveted to a chrome-plated steel rim. Even though the aluminum V-8 was 40 pounds lighter than the cast iron four in the MGB, the car was 167 pounds heavier at 2,427 pounds. Still, the car was capable of a top speed in the neighborhood of 125 miles per hour.

John Thornley was quoted as saying, "The MGB GT V-8 retained the weight, balance, and behavioral characteristics of the MGB with power roughly equivalent to that of the MGC. It was a very, very good motor car, so good in fact that it aroused a great deal of jealousy among competing factions

The second-generation MGB grille had a black crosshatch grille with the MG badge moved up into the chrome surround. One way of determining the vintage of your MGB is by the location of the "traveling" MG badge.

Rubber bumpers were included on the front and rear of 1975 and later MGBs. They were required to conform to federal regulations dictating no damage in an impact at five miles per hour or less.

within BL. Production was constantly interrupted by engine shortages and some of the decisions as to where, or more particularly where not, it should be marketed could not be explained in normal terms."

When Triumph decided to install the Rover V-8 in the dismal TR7 to give it some oomph, it was clear that the MG's V-8 days were numbered. During the V-8's production run, just 2,591 were built. In its first full year of production, 1973, 1,069 cars were built (after three were built in 1972), 854 were built in 1974, 489 in 1975, and 176 in 1976. One reason for the relatively low production numbers was a shortage of engines. Don Hayter said the most they could wheedle out of Rover was 48 in one week. Also, production coincided with the first Arab oil embargo, which saw fuel prices increase. Tentative plans to export the V-8 to the United States were abandoned. The car did have some appeal in Britain, though, as a police car.

The End

MG had seen numerous changes in its history. After starting life as a subsidiary of Morris Motors, it became successively a member of the British Motor Corporation, British Motor Holdings, and then British Leyland Motors. In 1977, when Michael Edwardes took over as chairman of British Leyland, the company's share of the market had dropped to 24 percent after having begun at nearly 90 percent. Part of the problem was the introduction of cars that simply weren't that good, such as the Triumph TR7, but the company was being run by Leyland people, so it was to Triumph that its attention was directed.

Edwardes responded to the lackluster sales of the TR7 by closing the plant in 1978. A year later, a meeting of BL's top management concluded that the workforce would have to be cut by 25,000, the Triumph factory at Canley would have to close, and MG production at Abingdon would have to cease. BL calculated that in 1979 it was losing £900 on every MGB it sold in the United States—its best market.

Hence, on September 10, 1979, the decision was announced to stop MG production. The last two MGBs were built on October 22, 1980. They were a bronze roadster, chassis number G-HN5 523001, and a pewter GT, chassis number G-HD5 523002.

Gearbox

The MGB was introduced with the always-frustrating four-speed manual gearbox with synchromesh on the top three gears only. In October 1967, an all-synchronized gearbox appeared, which made driving the B much simpler. How do you tell the difference? With the three-speed-synchronized box, there is a step down in the transmission tunnel to the rear of the gear lever; with the all-synchronized gearbox, the transmission tunnel has no step and runs smoothly toward the rear of the car. Most cars also have overdrive on the top two gears.

Problems can arise with worn bearings and damaged gears. These faults can be found by simply listening to the gearbox in operation, and the problem is most prevalent with the three-synchro unit. These transmissions are always noisy in first and reverse in cars where the owners drove as if the gearbox was all-synchro and ground into first or reverse when the car was moving.

Check for wear with the universal joints at both ends of the driveshaft. They tend to wear and this wear can be felt and heard.

A Borg Warner Type 35 automatic transmission was available on the B, but fewer than 1,800 cars were so equipped.

If you're rebuilding the engine, it's a good idea to rebuild the transmission, too.

The most obvious feature of the last MGBs was the rubber front bumper. The black polyurethane overbumper extended the length of the car by 6 inches (153.2 inches to 159.2 inches) and completely eliminated any semblance of an MG grille.

Chassis

There are two weaknesses in the otherwise strong suspension: the U-bolts on the rear leaf springs can work loose causing rear-end steering, and the front kingpins can wear, tending to make the steering sticky. The brakes and steering typically, however, present no major problems other than normal wear and tear.

Check for suspension modifications, which can improve handling. Again, it depends on why you're restoring the car—to make it as original as possible or to re-create a good runner. Front shock conversion to telescopic units from the lever-arm units is common as are rear sway bars, stiffer front sway bars, and stiffer suspension bushings.

Body

Some writers have said that the best way to determine the quality of a prospective MGB purchase is to examine the body closely, as this is the area that will require the most time and money to correct. A good body and bad mechanicals can be repaired in time; a good car mechanically that has a rusted body will have to be stripped to the frame someday and rebuilt.

MG introduced a Limited Edition MGB in 1980 that had as standard features a padded steering wheel, luggage rack, air dam under the big black bumper, and special badging and side stripes.

Check the sills. They not only provide the body's structural strength, they're also the first parts to rust. There are only seven panels per sill, but a lot of labor is required to replace them. Since each sill extends behind the front and rear fenders, the front fender and the lower part of the rear fender must be removed to replace them.

Also, check any areas that have been repainted poorly in an attempt to cover up rust or a poor restoration. A good place to check is the vertical seam below the front of the door. The sill profile should be slightly bowed, not straight. Also check for tapering door gaps, which indicate a poor rebuild.

All four fenders are likely to rust around the arches, on the bottom edge, along the top beading, and around lap housings.

Tops

The original top was made of ICI Everflex, which was a hard-wearing cloth-backed plastic with a deep grain. Three types of top were offered: a fully stowable type, an early folding top with a frame that can pinch holes in the fabric, and a folding type used after 1970 and designed by Michelotti, which is the best.

Wheels

Many restored Bs have wire wheels, which were always optional. Any movement from the wheels is an indication of worn splines or broken spokes. Wire-wheeled cars use a shorter rear axle, but there are conversion kits to convert back to the original rear axle ratio. And while you'll more than likely find chromed wire wheels, they were only an option between 1965 and 1971.

Restoration

The MGB is probably the easiest MG to buy and own, considering the number built and the availability of spare parts. While the

Mark I MGBs still had fairly uncomplicated engine compartments. In the Limited Edition, however, the impact of federal emissions legislation can be seen with the addition of various tubing, wiring, an air injection pump, PCV valve, and other hardware required to reduce emissions.

choice of roadster or GT is left up to the buyer, the first consideration must be in the condition of the body. The logic behind this choice is that the mechanical side of the car can be repaired fairly easily, but the body is what will take the most time and money and it's also the part of the car most people will see. Some estimates are that it costs 10 times as much to restore a body as it does to restore an engine.

To start, check the undersides of the doors for rust or paint blistering, which is the first sign of rust. There are seven panels involved in the sill area, but replacing them requires the front fender and windshield to be removed. All four fenders tend to rust around the arches, around the bottom edges, along the top beading, and where lights are fitted. Inner fender liners can also rust. The back of the front wheel arches should contain splash shields. At the front of the front wheel arches is a strengthening box section where mud can gather, aiding the formation of rust.

Doors also rust along the bottom edge, and sometimes split just below the wing window because of internal stresses. The hood shouldn't rust, because it was aluminum until 1969. If there is rust, you may have a post-1969 car. Floor pans and the trunk floor are also rust catchers. We know of one well-maintained MGB with no floor now. Check the trunk floor with the spare wheel removed for rust. Lift the edges of the carpets inside to see if the floor pan is rotting near the transmission tunnel.

Body shells are available from British Motor Industry Heritage Trust, and while they're built on MGB forms, they also use modern zinc-dipping methods to inhibit rust formation. The

In the Limited Edition, buyers got a padded steering wheel rim along with a redesigned instrument panel. The 1980 MGB LE was priced at $7,950 compared to $6,550 for the standard 1979 model.

Part of the paraphernalia that should be present on any MGB LE you are considering is this identification plate attached to the glovebox door.

BMC B-series 1,798-cc engine used in the MGB should last for 130,000 miles with good care. The best engines are those built after October 1964, which have the five-bearing crankshaft. MG engines have always been easy to work on and responsive to good care. Potential buyers of MGBs should check for oil and water leaks and for possible intermixing of oil and water, which would indicate a bad head gasket. Listen for noises and look for exhaust smoke. Of particular

importance are the oil pressure and water temperature gauges. Oil pressure should be at 50-65 psi when the engine is warm.

The transmission underwent only one major change—from synchromesh on the top three gears only to an all-synchromesh box in October 1967. In addition, most cars have overdrive on the top gears, especially if it's an American car. The clutch is strong and it should be; the engine has to be removed to replace it. Drive the car and listen for chunking from the rear end, which means the axle, drive shaft, or universal joints may need repair soon.

In the suspension area, the MGB will wander if the kingpins aren't greased regularly. Also, the U-bolts holding the rear springs can work loose, leading to rear-wheel steering effects. The lever-action rear shock absorbers are often replaced with telescopic type. Disc wheels are always a safer option than the optional wire wheels, simply because older wire wheels could easily go out of alignment.

MGBs on the Road

Unlike the MGA, the power curve on the MGB decreased over time. Later MGB engines, while still the same 1.8-liter capacity, dropped from the 95 horsepower of the original 1962 car to 62.5 horsepower for the 1980 model, a 34 percent decrease. The reason for the loss of power was, of course, emissions controls which strangled the engine.

Along with the loss of power, the cars gained weight as well, primarily because of safety legislation that dictated stronger bumpers and support structures.

Therefore, the earlier MGBs are probably better cars to drive, simply because of a more optimal power-to-weight ratio. They are still hampered by the lack of a fully synchronized gearbox, but an original MGB can be a fun car to drive, and can be as enjoyable as a Mazda Miata.

The argument of coupe versus roadster put forth for the MGA is less restrictive for the MGB. The latter car was designed with wind-up windows, making the MGB roadster a far

MG offered the "Limited Edition" of the rubber-bumper car, but it also offered a standard version of the car. This car is an example of the last MGBs offered.

Despite the apparent ungainliness of the rubber bumpers, race driver Terry Visger drove a Huffaker Engineering-prepared MGB to three consecutive SCCA E Production National Championships from 1975 to 1977.

better all-weather car than the MGA was.

For long-distance travel, however, the MGB/GT would be a better choice, if only because the hatchback of the GT offers far more luggage capacity than does the trunk of the roadster. Without air conditioning, though, the GT can be almost as stuffy and confining as the MGA coupe in summer, although there is better airflow inside the car for cooling.

A modern road test of a 1965 MGB in *Classic & Sportscar* noted: "The rod forming the rearview mirror support seems to split the screen in half, making it reminiscent of early postwar cars, and there's chrome everywhere. The view from the cockpit down the tapering bonnet makes it easy to judge distances and avoid the potholes that all too easily catch the B's suspension.

"Turn into a bend and the B leans noticeably, with more than a touch of understeer, and the steering loads up. You need to allow for the brakes, too, and the lack of synchromesh on first can be annoying. No, these things aren't perfect, but again the compensations are real enough."

Both the MGC and the Austin-Healy 3000 employed 3.0-liter, six-cylinder engines, but the MG unit was both smaller and lighter. Donald Healey had been offered an opportunity to badge-engineer an Austin-Healey after the MGC, but declined.

Specifications

MGB
Production dates: 5/1962–1977
Total production: 115,898
Chassis numbers: G-HN3101
Engine numbers:
Price: $2,568 (1962 POE)–$7,950 (1980 POE)
Engine:

      Type: Cast iron overhead valve inline four cylinder
      Displacement: 1,798 cc
      Bore: 80.26 mm
      Stroke: 88.9 mm
      Compression ratio: 8.8:1
      BHP: 95 @ 5,400 rpm
      Torque: 110 ft-lbs @ 3,000 rpm
      Red line: 6,000 rpm

Transmission:

      Type: Four-speed manual with synchromesh on top three gears
      Overall gear ratios:

4th*	3.9:1
3rd*	5.343:1
2nd*	8.619:1
1st	14.196:1
Reverse	18.59:1

           *Synchromesh
      Rear axle ratio: 3.9:1
      Clutch: 8-in Borg and Beck, single dry-plate diaphragm

Chassis:

      Type: Integral with steel body
      Wheels and tires: Ventilated 4Jx14 disc wheels, 4.5J wire wheels optional
      Tire size: 5.60x14
      Brakes: Lockheed hydraulic disc front, drum rear
      Electrical: Two 6-volt batteries
      Front suspension: Independent with coil springs and wishbones, Armstrong lever-action shock absorbers form the top link
      Rear suspension: Live axle with semielliptic leaf springs and Armstrong lever-action shock absorbers
      Fuel system: Twin SU 1-in Type HS4 carburetors
      Fuel tank: 12 gal
      Dimensions:

           Wheelbase: 91.0 in
           Overall length: 153.2 in
           Track front: 49.0 in
           Track rear: 49.25 in
           Width: 59.9 in
           Height: 49.4 in

Ground clearance: 4.5 in
Curb weight: 2,072 lbs

Colors:

Exterior: Flame Red, Bronze Yellow, British Racing Green, Blue Royale, Pale Primrose, Glacier White

Interior: Black, tan

Significant Modifications:

Chassis number G-HN3 101: First MGB; January 1963: Laycock overdrive became available, offering a final drive ratio of 3.12:1 in fourth and 4.29:1 in third. June 1963: Factory-approved hardtop became available

Chassis number G-HN3 31021: Closed-circuit crankcase breathing system

Chassis number G-HN3 48766: Five-bearing engine introduced; oil cooler became standard; mechanical speedometer replaced by electronic unit

Chassis number G-HN3 56743: Fuel tank capacity increased to 12 gal; mounting arrangement changed from two straps to securing bolts

Chassis number G-HN3 57986: Door handles altered, push button models introduced; locks and internal door mechanisms changed

Chassis number G-HD3 71933: GT model introduced

Chassis number G-HN3 108039: Front anti-roll bar fitted to Roadster

Chassis number G-HN3 132923 (wire-wheeled cars) and 139215 (disc wheel cars): Salisbury-type rear axle introduced on Roadster.

Chassis number G-HN4 138401 (Roadster) and G-HD4 139472 (GT): Chassis number prefix changed to reflect introduction of Mark II MGB; alternator installed in place of generator, changing grounding to negative; pre-engaged starter installed; gearbox tunnel enlarged; U.S.-spec cars fitted with emission control equipment

Chassis number G-HN5 187211 (Roadster) and G-HD5 187841 (GT): Chassis prefix numbers changed to reflect introduction of fifth series MGB; new recessed radiator grille introduced with chrome surround and MG badge located in the center; small British Leyland badges attached just forward of the doors; bumper overriders on U.S.-spec cars fitted with rubber inserts; Rostyle wheels introduced; interior included new reclining seats, vinyl upholstery, smaller three-spoke steering wheel

Chassis number G-HN5-219001: New top design introduced; telescopic hood and trunk lid supports; interior trunk light added; heating and ventilation system improved

Chassis number G-HN5/G-HD5 258001: Swivelling fresh air ducts added to previous radio location; radio relocated to a new console below the dash; rocker switches replaced tumbler switches. collapsible, energy-absorbing steering wheel extended to MGs sold in non-U.S. markets

Chassis number G-HN5 294251/G-HD5 296001: Radiator grill became black mesh with a chrome surround; leather-wrapped steering wheel and shift lever knob introduced; cigar lighter standard; windshield wipers black instead of chrome

Chassis number G-HN5/G-HD5 328101: Under-hood layout made common with the V-8; radial tires made standard; automatic gearbox option withdrawn; cars sold in the United States fitted with vertical rubber overriders

Chassis number G-HN5 360301/G-HD5 361001(UK)/G-HD5 363082 (US): Black polyurethane bumpers introduced; Roadster's ride height increased; GT withdrawn from American market; hazard warning lights added; door mirrors and power-assisted brakes made standard; overdrive unit changed to LH type; twin 6-volt batteries replaced by a single 12-volt source

     Chassis number G-HN5 410001: Front anti-roll bar thickened; rear anti-roll bar made standard; interior revamped; overdrive switch incorporated in the gear lever knob; new four-spoke steering wheel; lower gear steering introduced; engine cooling system sealed; fuel tank capacity reduced to 11 gal

     Chassis number G-HN5 522581/G-HD5 522422: Limited Edition model introduced

     Chassis number G-HN5 523001 (Roadster) and G-HD5 523002 (GT): Last MGBs built

Driver's Handbook factory part number: AKD3258A

Workshop Manual factory part number: AKD3294A

Parts List factory part number: AKD3227

MGC

Production dates: 1967–1969

Total production: 4,542

Chassis numbers: G/CN1

Engine numbers: N/A

Price: $3,350 POE—Roadster; $3,715—GT

Engine:

     Type: Water-cooled o.h.v. six-cylinder inline

     Displacement: 2,912 cc

     Bore: 83.362 mm

     Stroke: 88.9 mm

     Compression ratio: 9:1

     BHP: 145 @ 5,250 rpm

     Torque: 174 ft-lbs @ 3,500 rpm

     Red line: 6,000 rpm

Transmission:

     Type: BMC four-speed all-synchromesh with central remote-control gear lever; three-speed automatic

     Clutch: 9-in Borg and Beck single dry-plate diaphragm

     Overall gear ratios: (pre-1969 non-overdrive)

4th*	1.0:1
3rd*	1.382:1
2nd*	2.167:1
1st	3.44:1
Reverse:	2.67:1

     Overall gear ratios: (1969 non-overdrive)

4th*	1.0:1
3rd*	1.307:1
2nd*	2.058:1
1st	2.98:1
Reverse	2.67:1

     Overall gear ratios (overdrive)

4th*	0.82:1
3rd*	1.07:1
2nd*	2.058:1
1st	2.98:1
Reverse	2.67:1

Overall gear ratios (automatic)

        Top   3.31:1

        2nd   4.79:1

        3rd   7.91:1

        Reverse 2.67:1

        *Synchromesh

Rear axle ratio: 3.31:1

Non-overdrive to chassis 4235: 3.07:1

Overdrive cars to chassis 4235 and non-overdrive cars from chassis 4236: 3.31:1

Automatic gearbox: 3.31:1

Overdrive cars from chassis 4236: 3.7:1

Chassis:

Type: Unibody steel chassis

Wheels: 5Jx15 disc, 5J wire wheels optional

Steering: Rack and pinion

Tire size: 165R15

Brakes: Hydraulic servo-assisted 11-1/16-in discs front, 9-in drums rear

Front suspension: Torsion bars with antiroll bar and telescopic shock absorbers

Rear suspension: Semielliptic leaf springs controlled by lever-type

Electrical: Two 6-volt batteries

Fuel system: Twin SU type HS6 horizontal carburetors with one-piece aircleaner

Fuel tank: 12 gal

Dimensions:

        Wheelbase: 91.0 in

        Overall length: 153.2 in

        Track front: 50.0 in

        Track rear: 49.5 in

        Width: 60.0 in

        Height: 50.0 in

        Ground clearance: 4.5 in

        Curb weight: 2,604 lbs

        shock absorbers

Colors: Same as MGB

Significant chassis modifications:

        Chassis number G-CN 4236: Cars fitted with overdrive had their rear axle ratios changed from 3.31:1 to 3.7:1, and non-overdrive models changed from 3.07:1 to 3.31:1; 1969 model year: Close-ratio gearbox installed, Rostyle wheels installed on cars intended for export, reclining seats standardized.

        Chassis number G-CN 9099 (Roadster) and G-CD 9102 (GT): last MGCs built.

MGB/GT V-8

Production dates: 12/72–9/76

Total production: 2,802

Chassis numbers: GD2D1/101–GD2D1/1956 (chrome bumper); GD2D1/2101–GD2D1/2903

Engine numbers: 4860-0001 to 4860-2596

Engine:

        Type: Rover 3.5-liter aluminum V-8

        Displacement: 3,528 cc

        Bore: 88.90 mm

        Stroke: 71.12 mm

        Compression ratio: 8.25:1

        BHP: 137 @ 5,000 rpm

        Torque: 193 ft-lbs @ 2,900 rpm

Transmission:

        Type: Four-speed all synchromesh with overdrive on fourth

        Clutch: 9.5-inch Borg and Bech diaphragm type

        Overall gear ratios:

Overdrive	0.82:1
4th	1.000:1
3rd	1.259:1
2nd	1.974:1
1st	3.138:1
Reverse	3-138:1

        Rear axle ratio: 3.071:1

Chassis:

        Type: Monocoque, front engine, rear drive

        Wheels: 5Jx14 composite aluminum center with steel rims

        Tires: 175x14HR

        Brakes: 10.7-in discs front, 10-in drums rear

        Steering: Rack and pinion

        Front suspension: Independent with coil springs and lower wishbone mounted on cross-member assembly. Lever-type shock absorbers and anti-roll bar

        Rear suspension: Tube type live axle with three-quarter floating drive shafts. Semielliptic multiple leaf springs. Lever-type shock absorbers. Fuel system: Twin SU HIF6 carburetors

        Fuel tank: 12 gal

        Dimensions:

            Wheelbase: 91.125 in

            Overall length: 154.75 in (chrome bumper) 158.25 in (rubber bumper)

            Track front: 49.0 in

            Track rear: 49.25 in

            Width: 59.94 in

            Height: 49.96 in

            Curb weight: 2,427 pounds

Colors:

        Exterior: Aconite, black, Black Tulip, Blaze, Bracken, Bronze Yellow, Brooklands Green, chartreuse, citron, Damask Red, Flamenco Red, Glacier White, Green Mallard, Harvest Gold, Limeflower, Mirage, Police White, Sandglow, Tahiti Blue, Teal Blue, tundra

        Interior: Navy, ochre, black, Autumn Leaf

Significant modifications:
    Chassis number G-D2D1 101: First MGB GT V-8
    Chassis number G-D2D1 2903: Last MGB GT V-8

Production:	Year	MGB	MGB/GT	Total	MGC	MGC/GT
	1962	4,518	4,518			
	1963	23,308	23,308			
	1964	26,542	26,542			
	1965	24,179	524	24,703		
	1966	22,675	10,241	32,916		
	1967	15,128	11,396	26,524	189	41
	1968	17,355	8,352	25,707	2,566	2,462
	1969	19,050	12,212	31,262	1,789	1,954
	1970	23,644	12,462	36,106		
	1971	22,444	12,110	34,554	MGB/V-8	
	1972	26,192	13,174	39,366	3	
	1973	19,565	10,218	29,783	1,069	
	1974	18,966	9,581	28,547	854	
	1975	19,966	4,609	24,575	489	
	1976	25,860	3,698	29,558	176	
	1977	24,490	4,191	28,681		
	1978	22,006	5,658	27,664		
	1979	19,897	3,473	23,370		
	1980	11,004	3,424	14,428		
Totals		386,789	125,323	512,112		

Note: of these numbers, 336,979 Roadsters (87 percent) and 60,416 GTs (48 percent) were built for export, or a total of 397,395 or 77.6 percent.

Production:	Year	MGC	MGC/GT	Total
	1967	189	41	230
	1968	2,566	2,462	5,028
	1969	1,787	1,954	3,741
	Total	4,5424,457		8,999

MGB/V-8	
1972	3
1973	1,069
1974	854
1975	489
1976	176
Total	2,592

★★★✦	MG Midget 1500
★★★	MG Midget Mark I
★★★	MG Midget Mark III
★★	MG Midget Mark IV
★	MG Midget Mark II

Midgets

With the success of the "Bugeye" Austin Healey Sprite, BMC did what any self-respecting car manufacturer would do; it badge-engineered another model. Coincidental with the introduction of the 1962 Mark II Sprite, MG introduced the "Mark I" MG Midget in June 1961. The cute little Midget, while it claimed the name of Midgets of the past, was a modern version of the same. It was a small sports car with decent performance for its size. The fact that it was essentially identical to the second-generation Sprite didn't hurt. As manufacturers have known for decades, if people want an Austin Healey, they'll buy a Sprite; if they want an MG, they'll buy a Midget, even if it's the same car. After the Sprite was dropped by British Leyland, all responsibility for the design of the car, known affectionately as the Spridget, rested with MG. There was no rubber bumper version of the Sprite as there was for the MG.

Initially, the Midget was powered by a 948-cc inline four that was a derivative of the Morris Minor sedan engine. The 46-horsepower engine drove the rear wheels through a four-speed manual gearbox. A high-compression head was soon available that would increase horsepower to 50. MG fans were happy to see a new Midget, and it was the first MG with an engine of under 1-liter capacity since the PB of 1936. Most of the motoring press liked the Midget more than the more stark Sprite.

While capable of a top speed of only 85–90 miles per hour, the Midget was a worthy small sports car. It offered all the fun and charm of the larger MGs, but at a much better price. And the smaller engine also delivered better fuel economy.

The drivetrain was enclosed in a very MG-like body, with a grille composed of vertical chrome slats that was not unlike what the future MGB grille would look like. There was also a small carpeted area behind the front seats that might hold a (very) small child or some luggage. All this was available for a list price of just under $2,000 ($1,939 to be exact). It was a nice package and proved to be very popular. A total of 224,363 MG Midgets would be sold from 1962 until the final Mark IV version ceased production in 1979. It offered a package that the Mazda Miata would use to gain its own solid reputation in the 1990s, although the Miata is far better built than the Midget ever was.

MG Midgets under construction at Abingdon. The Midget proved to be a popular car, even though it was smaller than the MGB. In later years, the Midget would acquire a host of creature comforts, such as wind-up windows, that would make it a much more civilized automobile.

Mark I Midgets were styled with "MG-like" grilles with vertical chrome slats in a horizontal frame. The idea was to give the Midget more "style" than the more pedestrian Austin-Healey Sprite. Early Midgets also had disc wheels as standard, although wire wheels were more commonly seen in the United States.

Like its showroom floor mate, the MGB, the Midget went through a series of modifications through its life that would help it comply with federal emissions regulations and crash standards. Eventually, these regulations would prove to be the death of the car, as they would for the MGB. Beginning with the 948-cc engine of the Sprite, the Midget was underpowered. Shortly after its introduction, a higher compression (9.0:1 versus 8.3:1) head became available that increased power output from the original 46 horsepower to 50 horsepower. It was a small increase, but in a car that only weighed three-quarters of a ton, it was enough to improve performance.

The frame, like that of the Sprite before it, was built up of two side-members separated by a flat floor. A bracing member ran parallel to the side beams and held the

Mark I Midgets (and some early Mark II versions) still had the plastic side curtains that came with the original Austin-Healey Sprites. Even though the body style was different from the original Bug-eye Sprites, the side curtains remained essentially the same. It wasn't until the Mark II Midget that wind-up windows became available.

transmission tunnel. Another bracing formed what British writers call the scuttle (underneath the A-pillar), and two members reached forward from this point. In the rear was a box that formed the trunk. There was no trunk lid in the original Sprite; access was from inside the car. In the Midget, though, a proper trunk lid was fitted. Front fenders were now bolted to the chassis, unlike in the Sprite where they lifted with the hood to provide engine access. Rear styling allowed for large vertical light clusters that were not unlike those on the MGB.

Windows were not an option on the first Midgets; side screens were the order of the day. The Midget carried an MG-like grille, with vertical chrome strips surrounded by a chrome frame. But in all respects, it was little more than a luxury Sprite. The front suspension was derived from the Austin A30 sedan, with a large wishbone forming the lower link and a hydraulic lever-action shock absorber forming the upper link. A coil spring was between them. In the rear were stiff quarter elliptic springs with lever-action shock absorbers. The front of the springs were attached to the chassis and the rear attached to the axle mounting point. The

The Mark II Midget is especially noted because of its wind-up windows that replaced the plastic side curtains. In addition, the engine was now about 100 cc larger (1,098 cc). In order to stop this more powerful car, front disc brakes have been added, but the original chrome grille remained the same.

two bucket seats offered minimal legroom, but were covered by a soft top that stowed in the rear compartment. *Autocar* said it was immediately impressed by the smoothness of the Midget's engine, and praised its willingness to move the needle up the tachometer to the 6,000-rpm red line. The magazine did note, however, that the Midget was noisy above 70 miles per hour. As for handling, the Mark I Midget tended to oversteer, which was a result of the rear-wheel steering effect of the solid

The Mark II retained the original clean lines of the Mark I Midget, even with the addition of wing windows and headrests.

rear axle. On the other hand, extremely good bump absorption was provided by the suspension.

A fiberglass hardtop was available that required separate side screens. There was good draft sealing with either top in place, a testament to the efficiency of the new side screens and their aluminum frames with double sliding Perspex plastic windows. *Autocar* concluded its 1961 review by stating, "This new MG Midget is an endearing little car with a remarkable capacity for nipping about among heavy traffic. It is easy and safe to drive, and certainly is approaching the ideal for the market which it is intended to serve."

Mark I Second Version

A second version of the original car was introduced in October 1962 for the 1963 model year. Still called the Mark I (or,

technically, given no new identification) this car would have a 1,098-cc engine that delivered 55 horsepower, a solid 10-percent increase. MG decided to improve the stopping power with the going power, and added disc brakes to the hotter car.

But even though the engine was larger and delivered more power, the stroke was increased more than the bore and the long-stroke engine received bad reviews. With the larger engine came front disc brakes and an improved gearbox and better ratios. Wire wheels became an optional extra, although most cars sold in the United States were equipped with them.

With the increased power of the new engine (55 horsepower versus 46.6 horsepower), the inadequacies of the rear suspension showed up with a tendency to oversteer. A revised rear suspension appeared on the Mark II Midget (and Mark III Sprite).

Of course, the Midget was built under the British Leyland regime, so all badging reflected not only the fact that it was an MG, but also the fact that it was a "BL" car.

All Mark I Midgets after car No. 20208 were fitted with modified side screens that would not stick as much. Many Midget owners discovered that the felt channels in which the windows slid absorbed water in the rain and swelled, making the sliding action very stiff. Thinner felt was fitted to the later windows. Cars prior to No. 20208 could have the channels modified by the addition of thinner felt and two springs for each side.

The convertible top bows now separated in the middle, which made the top more difficult to put up and take down, but made it possible to stow the top in the trunk. As with all British cars, rust is a demon. Body rust can form in the seam on the front fenders just behind the wheel opening. Rust will tend to form in the lower panel of the fenders and in the pillar just below the windshield. The pillar rusts because the rubber seal under the windshield leaks, which allows water to run down into the chassis.

For an authentic 948-cc engine, look for the "950" cast into the side of the block. Also, the original engines used 1 1/2-inch SU carburetors, which are difficult to find. Later cars had these H1 models changed to HS2, 1 1/4-inch carbs.

Mark II

A true Mark II version of the Midget appeared in 1964. The engine was still the 1,098-cc four, but with a compression ratio increase to 9.0:1 that added another four horsepower, to 59. This increase was brought about by the installation of the head that had been used on the MG 1100 sedan. Since it was marketed concurrent with the MGB, the Mark II also had a few of the B's creature comforts: roll-up windows with vent windows, a taller, more curved windshield, and locking outside door handles. The pull starter was replaced with one that was integral with the ignition switch, and self-canceling turn signals were now standard.

In addition, the doors were different from the Mark I Midget, primarily to incorporate the wind-down windows, the cranking mechanism, and the wing windows. The new windshield had a central bracing rod, as with the MGB, and the rearview mirror was attached to this rod. The slightly wider doors meant that the interior had slightly less room.

Inside, there was a redesigned dash and a new three-spoke steering wheel with a central horn button. The speedometer and tachometer are located in front of the driver, with their dials tilted inward to face the driver. Other gauges include a fuel gauge and a combined oil pressure/water temperature gauge. These were mounted in the center and were well spaced with the minor controls to avoid any confusion. Under the dash on the passenger side was a rounding to provide easier entry for taller drivers. A parcel shelf was also included under the dash on the passenger side.

The standard wheels for the Mark II were bolt-on discs, but center-lock wire wheels were an option and were the choice found on most U.S.-spec cars. In the rear suspension, the quarter elliptic leaf springs were replaced with semielliptic springs, which resulted in an improvement in riding comfort as well as a reduction in road noise. The front of the spring was attached to the chassis, and the rear extended beyond the axle attachment point to the rear of the chassis. A regular rust spot on the cars that became affectionately known as "Spridgets"—a combination of "Sprite" and "Midget"— is the jacking point on the side,

The 1,098-cc engine in the Mark II Midget developed 55 horsepower. While this wasn' t an overwhelming amount of power, even for its time, the lightness of the Midget still allowed for spirited performance.

near the front of the door. Usually covered by a rubber plug that is often rotted away, this area is a rust magnet.

Another rust magnet is the area around the taillights. The rubber boot on the fuel filler neck is also prone to rot and can be replaced. Another rubber boot that often rots easily is the one at the base of the shift lever. It, too, is easily replaced.

Leather straps hold the doors and keep them from banging into the side panels when the doors are opened. Replacement is easy.

Mark III

The next significant change in the MG Midget was the Mark III version, which appeared in 1967. MG had experimented with an open version of the Mini, code-named ADO34, but it received no support from the BMC corporate offices. But Long-bridge did allow MG to use the 1,275-cc Mini engine in the Midget, which produced 65 horsepower when it was introduced. Compared with the 48 horses under the Mark I's hood, this was a big step. This engine was the same as that used in the Mini Cooper S, but detuned. Compression ratio was 8.8:1 and an air injection system was added to improve emissions. An oil cooler was also optional.

Initially, the cranks in the 1,275 engine were the same as those in the 1,100, and they tended to break. The first solution was to use a nitrided crank, as was used in the Mini. Later cranks were made from a different material and lasted longer.

On the chassis side, the folding top of the convertible no longer required the manual installation of bows and ribs. It was "semi-automatic." It folded back into a recess behind the seats, leaving a slight bit above the body that is covered by a tonneau.

Replacement tonneaus are expensive, as are the tops. Any that survive today are likely to have tears and cracked or scratched plastic windows. In addition, the storage area behind the cockpit that was designed to hold the top also took away from the storage capacity.

Standard equipment during the model's lifetime included twin horns, two-speed wipers with washers, backup lights, a heater/defroster, reclining Ambla vinyl bucket seats with headrests, three-point seatbelts, lighter, fitted carpeting, rubber floor mats, and padded sun visors. The standard wheels were mag-style Rostyle wheels, while wire wheels were an option.

Autocar said in its February 4, 1971, test that the top erection and removal were easier than on most British sports cars. The magazine felt that the Midget and Sprite (the Spridget twins) were ideal first sports car for a young person, since they offered excellent handling, decent styling, and enough power to have fun.

In 1972, the rounded rear wheel arches of the Midget were modified to flat-topped arches. In that year, too, the engine compression was reduced to 8.0:1 to reduce emissions and the dash now held a locking glovebox. For 1974, huge black padded bumper overriders were added. These were in response to crash legislation and would precede the "rubber baby buggy bumper" front end of the Mark IV.

Special tuning kits were available for the Mark III. These included new camshafts for full race or rallying; a specially hardened crankshaft; flat top pistons; larger valves; new cylinder head assembly, 1-inch SU carburetors; close ratio gears; 5-inch rims; 4.55:1 or 3.727:1 rear axle gears; limited slip differential; lowered rear road springs; lower front suspension kit; competition shock absorbers; sway bar; and competition brake pads.

Mark IV

The British Leyland Motor Corporation was formed in 1968 with Donald Stokes at its head. Stokes was apparently aware of Triumph and thought that marque was the only British sports car. And Triumph was

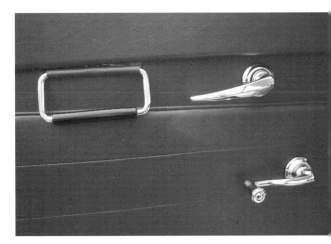

MG's have always relied on a certain amount of minimalism. Here, the Mark II midget has a proper crank for its wind-up windows, but offers only a simple pull handle for the door. They tend to wear out easily. I had a similar pull handle on my MGA coupe that pulled out of the inner door liner within a year.

building its own small sports car, the Spitfire. So it came as something of a surprise when the Mark IV Midget was announced.

The Midget's final iteration appeared in the 1975 model year. It was introduced at the October 1974 Motor Show. Production would continue into the summer of 1979. Oddly, since the Midget began its life as a clone of the Austin-Healey Sprite, it was the Mark IV Midget that was left to soldier on by itself, as the Sprite was dropped from the BLMC lineup.

The most obvious change to the Mark IV (or MG Midget 1500) was its huge nose of soft black polyurethane that replaced the chrome grille. The nose was another response to crash legislation. No grille was evident, although there was an MG octagon in the center. There was a matching bumper at the rear. The Mark IV also rode higher, thanks to a taller suspension. In the back, the rounded rear wheel openings replaced the flat-top style.

Two additional structural members were added to the body to provide support for the front bumper. The total weight went up 170 pounds, quite a bit on a small car. Federal regulations also dictated that the car

The last BMC engine available in the Midget was the 1,275-cc unit also available in the Mini. Later Midgets would use the 1,500-cc four-cylinder engine borrowed from the Triumph Spitfire, but MG purists don't consider this a true MG engine.

be raised, which caused considerable roll in cornering and made for sloppy handling. The engine was all-new and in a move that disturbed MG purists, it was borrowed from the Triumph Spitfire. MG was now a division of British Leyland and engines were shared across the line. The new 1,493-cc four used a single Zenith-Stromberg carburetor, rather than the twin SUs that had been standard from the beginning. Power was down to 55 horsepower in U.S. tune, but the new engine gave the Midget a top speed of over 100 miles per hour for the first time.

While MG fans felt that the installation of a Triumph engine in the Midget was a form of heresy, in truth the 1,275-cc engine had reached the end of its tether and really couldn't be improved any more. But the new engine gave the Midget considerably more potential than the 1,275 engine. One long-awaited change was the addition of synchromesh on first gear. MG was one of the last sports car manufacturers to make the move and it was a welcome one, especially since power levels were dropping on all cars and the ability to shift easily into first seemed more necessary. In its final year of production, the MG Midget, which had cost under $2,000 when it was introduced, carried a price tag of $5,200. But in that time the MGB price had also risen to $6,550, so the Midget was still a good bargain.

Mike Allison, in *MG: The Magic of the Marque*, stated, "I feel that the Midget had grown from 948 cc to 1,275 cc gracefully, but needed replacement at that juncture, when the design was 20 years old. Further development of the model on the same chassis was doomed. . . . The essential elements of the Midget were present as long as the old A-series engine was there, and it was capable of being tuned to give far better performance.

Later Midgets abandoned the vertical chrome strips of the original Midget in favor of a black mesh grille with a centralized MG badge. Rubber inserts were added to the bumpers in the first step of "bumper legislation" that would ultimately produce big polyurethane bumpers on the car. The top was "semi-automatic," meaning that the operator had to take it down manually and fold it back into a recess behind the seats, leaving a bit above the body. Jaguar's automatic top on the 1997 XK8 also rests a bit above the body line, for example.

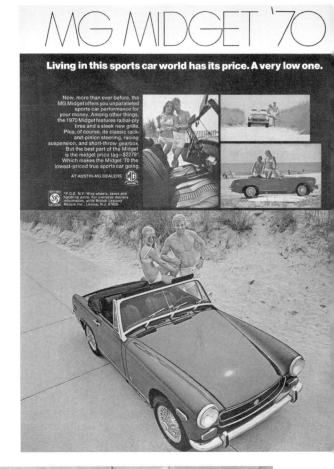

Like its big brother the MGB, the MG Midget also went to a rubber-bumper design to meet federal 5-mile-per-hour crash regulations. Many people considered these bumpers to be the reason for the death of the Midget and B.

The Midget was a sports car, and as such it was equipped with a full set of instruments. Primary among these were a tachometer and speedometer located right in front of the driver, with other accessory gauges mounted around the instrument panel.

The final engine for the Midget was a 1,500-cc unit that was also used in the Triumph Spitfire. MG realized that with the installation of the Triumph engine in an MG, the life of the MG was almost over, and production ceased shortly after this combination was introduced. Note use of single carbs versus previous dual carb setup.

Once the 1,500-cc engine was fitted, the performance was there immediately, but the engine was somehow 'softer' and less forgiving if driven really hard: this being the difference between the earlier Midget and the Spitfire, of course!"

Autocar tested the Midget 1500 in June 1975 and said that the engine was a good addition to the car, but the old suspension of double wishbones at the front and a live rear axle located by semielliptic leaf springs in the rear showed signs that "the latest car needs something more sophisticated to cope with its greater torque and performance." The real snag, according to *Autocar*, was in the Midget's sensitivity to the throttle.

In conclusion, *Autocar* said, "People are bound to differ on how badly cramped they find the interior (although few will argue with the infuriating difficulty of reaching the interior door handles). For our money, the Spitfire is much more practical and civilized. There will always be those who scorn it for precisely these reasons, but if further rationalization comes to pass it will be difficult to make out a case for the Midget vis-à-vis its stablemate."

And, in fact, the Spitfire would outlive the Midget, if only by a few years.

Gearbox

An improved gearbox was introduced with the Mark II Midget in 1963, along with an increase in engine displacement from 948 cc to 1,098 cc. It was not until 1974, when the 1,500-cc Triumph Spitfire engine was shoehorned into the Midget along with its transmission, that an all-synchromesh gearbox was available for the smallest MG. The Spitfire's all-synchromesh engine and gearbox gave the Midget a top speed of over 100 miles per hour for the first time, even with emissions controls added.

Chassis

The rear suspension on early Midgets was adequate for the underpowered little car. However, with the introduction of the 1,098-cc engine, the rear suspension's tendency to oversteer revealed itself. Therefore, concurrent with the introduction of the new engine came a rear suspension that incorporated semielliptic leaf springs, whereas the Mark I Midget's live axle used trailing quarter

Since the Midget was a small car (it did live up to its name), the optional trunk-mounted luggage rack was a definite asset that could increase carrying capacity.

elliptic leaf springs, radius arms, and lever-type shocks.

Brakes

Mark I Midgets came equipped with drum brakes all around. With the larger engine in the Mark II Midget came front disc brakes combined with optional wire wheels.

Body

The Midget, although derived from the Sprite, did not share the Mark I Sprite's fanciful "Bugeye" hood. Introduced with the Mark II Sprite in April 1961, the Mark I Midget had front fenders bolted to the chassis with a normal hood replacing the front-hinged Bugeye hood.

A revised body shell was introduced at the same time as the 1,275-cc engine in the Mark III Midget.

Tops

Like the original Sprite, the Mark I Midget retained the same style: a top and frame that stowed in the compartment behind the seats. Along with the revised body shell of the Mark III Midget came a folding top. A fiberglass hardtop was an optional extra.

Windows

The Mark I Midget, like the Sprite before it, used plastic side screens. Later Midgets would show a shift toward modernization with wind-up windows and wing windows.

Wheels

While disc wheels were standard and wire wheels were always an option with the MG Midget, the only wheels you're likely to find on a Midget today are wire wheels. The wire wheels served as a distinguishing feature between the Midget and its twin, the Austin-Healey Sprite, and, therefore, were commonly chosen and used in restorations.

A tonneau cover was a practical means of protecting the car if you didn't want to put the top up. Any articles left inside the car would remain dry in a rainstorm and wouldn't be subjected to the harsh glare of full sunlight.

Specification

MG MIDGET MK I
Production dates: 6/61–10/62
Total production: 16,080
Chassis numbers: GAN1/101-GAN1/16183
Engine numbers: **[????]**
Price: $1,939 (POE)
Engine:

> Type: Cast iron inline four cylinder
> Displacement: 948 cc
> Bore: 2.478 in
> Stroke: 3.00 in
> Compression ratio: 8.3:1 (later 9.0:1)
> BHP: 46 @ 5,500 rpm (later 50 @ 5,500 rpm)
> Torque: (later 53 ft-lbs @ 4,000 rpm)
> Red line: 6,000 rpm

Transmission:

> Type: Four-speed manual
> Clutch: Dry clutch
> Overall gear ratios:
>> 4th*   1.00:1
>> 3rd*   1.357:1
>> 2nd*   1.916:1
>> 1st   3.20:1 (3.63:1 or 2.93:1 also available)
>> Reverse: 4.114:1
>> *Synchromesh
> Rear axle ratio: 4.22:1

Chassis:

> Type: Steel unibody
> Wheels: Four-stud ventilated disc
> Tires: Dunlop 5.20x13
> Brakes: Lockheed hydraulic 7-in front and rear drums
> Front suspension: Independent wishbones and coil springs with lever shocks and anti-roll bar
> Rear suspension: Trailing arms and quarter elliptic leaf springs with lever shocks
> Steering: Rack and pinion
> Fuel system: Two semidowndraft SU carburetors
> Fuel tank: 7.2 gal
> Dimensions:
>> Wheelbase: 80.0 in
>> Overall length: 136.0 in
>> Track front: 45.8 in
>> Track rear: 44.8 in
>> Width: 53.0 in
>> Height: 49.8 in
>> Ground clearance: 5.0 in
>> Curb weight: 1,566 lbs

Colors:

        Exterior: Tartan Red, Clipper Blue, Farina Gray, Old English White, black

        Interior: Red, black, dark blue

Driver's Handbook factory part number: AKD1774D

Workshop Manual factory part number: AKD1775B

Parts List factory part number: AKD1879

MG MIDGET MARK I (Second version)

Production dates: 1964–1966

Total production: 9,601

Chassis numbers: GAN2/16184-GAN2/25787

Engine numbers:

Price: $1,939

Engine:

        Type: Cast iron inline four cylinder

        Displacement: 1,098 cc

        Bore: 64.6 mm

        Stroke: 83.7 mm

        Compression ratio: 8.9:1

        BHP: 59 @ 5,500 rpm

        Torque: 61 ft-lbs @ 2,500 rpm

        Red line: 6,000 rpm

Transmission:

        Type: Four-speed manual

        Clutch: Dry clutch

        Overall gear ratios:

                4th*   1.00:1

                3rd*   1.357:1

                2nd*   1.916:1

                1st   3.20:1 (also 3.63:1 or 2.93:1)

                Reverse 4.114:1

                *Synchromesh

        Rear axle ratio: 4.22:1

Chassis:

        Type: Steel unibody

        Wheels: Four-stud ventilated discs

        Tires: Dunlop 5.20x13

        Brakes: Front disc/Rear drum

        Steering: Rack and pinion

        Front suspension: Wishbones and coil springs with lever shock absorbers

        Rear suspension: Trailing arms and quarter elliptic leaf springs with lever shock absorbers

        Fuel system: Twin SU semidowndraft carburetors

        Fuel tank: 7.2 gal

        Dimensions:

                Wheelbase: 80.0 in

                Overall length: 137.8 in

                Track front: 45.8 in

                Track rear: 44.8 in

Width: 53.0 in
Height: 49.8 in
Ground clearance: 5.0 in
Curb weight: 1,456 lbs
Colors: Same as Mark I Midget

MG MIDGET MK II

Production Dates: Early 1964–late 1966
Total production: 26,601
Chassis numbers: GAN3/25788-GAN3/52389
Engine numbers: 10CC/Da/H101
Price: $1,945 (POE)
Engine:

Type: Cast iron inline four
Displacement: 1,098 cc
Bore: 64.6 mm
Stroke: 83.7 mm
Compression ratio: 9.0:1
BHP: 59 @ 5,750 rpm
Torque: 61 ft-lbs @ 3,250 rpm
Red line: 6,000 rpm

Transmission:

Type: Four-speed manual
Clutch: Dry clutch
Overall gear ratios:

4th*   1.00:1
3rd*   1.357:1
2nd*   1.916:1
1st   3.20:1 (3.63:1 or 2.93:1 available)
Reverse: 4.114:1
*Synchromesh

Rear axle ratio: 4.22:1

Chassis:

Type: Steel unibody, front engine rear drive
Wheels: Four-stud ventilated discs, wire wheels available
Tires: Dunlop 5.20x13
Brakes: Lockheed front disc/rear drum
Steering: Rack and pinion
Front suspension: Wishbones and coil springs with lever-action shock absorbers
Rear suspension: Rigid axle with semielliptic leaf springs and lever shock absorbers
Fuel system: Two semidowndraft SU carburetors
Fuel tank: 7.2 gal
Dimensions:

Wheelbase: 80.0 in
Overall length: 137.8 in
Track front: 45.8 in
Track rear: 44.8 in
Width: 53.0 in

Height: 49.8 in
Ground clearance: 5.0 in
Curb weight: 1,566 lbs

Colors:

Exterior: Tartan Red, Riviera Blue, British Racing Green, Old English White, Dove Gray, black, Fiesta Yellow, Pale Primrose Yellow

Interior: Red, black, light blue

MG MIDGET MARK III

Production dates: 10/1966–late 1974
Total production: 99,896
Chassis numbers: GAN5UA74886–GAN5UE174752
Engine numbers: 12CC/Da/101
Price: $2,174 (POE 1967)
Engine:

Type: Cast iron inline four cylinder
Displacement: 1,275 cc
Bore: 70.6 mm
Stroke: 81.3 mm
Compression ratio: 8.8:1
BHP: 65 @ 6,000 rpm
Torque: 72 ft-lbs @ 3,000 rpm
Red line: 6,000 rpm

Transmission:

Type: Four-speed manual
Clutch: Borg and Beck diaphragm spring 6.5-in diameter
Overall gear ratios:

4th*	1.00:1
3rd*	1.357:1
2nd*	1.916:1
1st	3.20:1
Reverse	4.114:1

*Synchromesh

Rear axle ratio: 4.22:1 (others available)
Chassis:

Type: Steel unibody, front engine, rear drive
Wheels: Four-stud ventilated disc, wire wheels optional
Tires: Dunlop 5.20x13
Brakes: Lockheed front disc/rear drum
Steering: Rack and pinion
Front suspension: Wishbones and coil springs with lever-action shock absorbers
Rear suspension: Rigid axle with semielliptic leaf springs and lever shock absorbers
Fuel system: Two SU semidowndraft carburetors
Fuel tank: 7.5 gal
Dimensions:

Wheelbase: 80.0 in
Overall length: 137.6 in
Track front: 46.3 in

Track rear: 44.8 in
Width: 54.9 in
Height: 48.6 in
Ground clearance: 5.0 in
Curb weight: 1,512 lbs

Colors:

Exterior: Tartan Red, Basilica Blue, British Racing Green, Old English White, black, Pale Primrose Yellow, Mineral Blue, Glacier White
Interior: Black, red

MG MIDGET MARK IV

Production dates: 10/74–8/79
Total production: 72,185
Chassis numbers: GAN6UG166301G–GAN6UJ/238486G
Price: $3,549 (POE 1975)
Engine:

Type: Cast iron inline four (from Triumph Spitfire)
Displacement: 1,493 cc
Bore: 73.7 mm
Stroke: 87.5 mm
Compression ratio: 9.1:1
BHP: 55 @ 5,000 rpm
Torque: 67 ft-lbs @ 2,500 rpm
Red line: 6,000 rpm

Transmission:

Type: Four-speed all synchromesh
Clutch: Diaphragm spring, 7.25-in diameter

Overall gear ratios:

4th*	1.00:1
3rd*	1.433:1
2nd*	2.112:1
1st*	3.412:1
Reverse	3.75:1

*Synchromesh

Rear axle ratio: 3.90:1

Chassis:

Type: Steel unibody

Wheels: 4.5Jx13

Tires: 145x13 radial

Brakes: Front disc/rear drum

Steering: Rack and pinion

Front suspension: Wishbones and coil springs with lever shock absorber, anti-roll bar optional

Rear suspension: Rigid axle with semielliptic leaf springs and lever shock absorbers

Fuel system: Single Zenith CD4 carburetor

Fuel tank: 8.5 gal

Dimensions:

Wheelbase: 80.0 in

Overall length: 141.0 in

Track front: 46.3 in

Track rear: 44.8 in

Width: 54.0 in

Height: 48.3 in

Ground clearance: 5.0 in

Curb weight: 1,854 lbs

Colors:

Exterior: Brooklands Green, chartreuse, Damask Red, Flamenco, Glacier White, Sand-glow, Tahiti Blue

Interior: Autumn Leaf, black

★★★★	YA/YB
★★★✦	YT
★★★	ZA Magnette
★★★	ZB Magnette
★★	MG 1100/1300
★★	Magnette Mark III/IV

MG Sedans

After World War II, MG produced sedans with three basic body designs. First among these were the Y-Type (also known as the One and a Quarter Litre) and the Z Magnette. The Y-Type was based on the TD and the Magnette on the MGA. Both the Y-Type and the Z Magnette were adaptations of the sports car chassis with a four-door sedan body attached. (I was particularly smitten by the Z Magnette when I owned an MGA, but I couldn't convince my wife that it was a winner.)

MG also offered a badged version of the BMC 1100, which it called the MG 1100, as a successor to the Mini. This compact sedan had a transverse-mounted 1,100-cc engine that drove the front wheels. It was housed in a boxy four-door sedan package that was not unattractive. Again, I couldn't convince my wife of its merits.

What was unique about the 1100 was its "Hydrolastic Suspension," designed by Alec Issigonis. This was a unique approach to

MG produced the WA sedan just prior to World War II, but ceased production upon the onset of hostilities. The WA was a large sedan and definitely prewar in style, with a long hood, short trunk area, and sweeping fenders. *Plain English Archive*

MG's first postwar sedan was the Y-Type, which used the T-series underpinnings. Also known as the 1 1/4-Litre because of its engine capacity, it had an independent front suspension, which was rare for the time. Although the 1,250-cc engine only used one carburetor, versus the two carburetors found in the TC, the Y-Type was a peppy little sedan. It was also produced as an open four-seater and as a two-door tourer model. *Plain English Archive*

suspending automobiles that worked for a while, although it was never adopted by other manufacturers. Walt Hansgen even drove an "MG Hydrolastic Suspension" car in the Indianapolis 500 in 1964 (finished 12th) and 1965 (DNF).

Unlike Jaguar, where sedan production has always provided the resources for the company to produce exciting sports cars, MG was a sports car manufacturer that dabbled in sedan production. The cars sold reasonably well—some models reached 200,000 sales—but they were never the mainstay. When "the going got tough" in the late 1970s, it was the sedans that were dropped.

Among these cars, only the ZA and ZB Magnettes and the MG 1100 and MG 1300 were imported to the United States. While the Y-Types and Mark III and Mark IV sold well in Britain, they were never sold in the United States.

After MG ceased producing sports cars in 1979, the company began producing a line of high-performance small sedans under the Metro name. These were never imported to the United States, although they enjoyed some success in Europe and brought MG's name back to the fore in international rallies.

Y (YA/YT)

Before World War II, MG had produced three sedans, the VA (1-liter), the SA (2-liter), and the WA (2.6 liter). All were decent sedans, well-built and of high quality in the medium price range. Immediately after the war, MG concentrated on the TC Midget. Sedan production was put on hold, although plans were afoot for what an MG sedan might be like. In the spring of 1947, the YA was announced, using the same 1 1/4-liter engine that was being used in the TC, although with one carburetor. Also known as the MG 1 1/4-liter, the YA had definite prewar styling.

The YA was a medium-priced, luxuriously finished four-door sedan of compact

The Y-Type was well-received when it was introduced in the spring of 1947. Up front was an independent front suspension, which was rare in England at the time. The car had a welded, box-section chassis that was underslung at the rear, and rack-and-pinion steering. *Margaret Harrison*

dimensions. It was by no means roomy inside, but it had a stiff box-section frame, independent front suspension, and rack-and-pinion steering. And, it could cruise at 70 miles per hour.

In 1948, MG introduced for export only the YT, a two-door tourer version of the YA that used a two-carburetor version of the engine. Only about 1,000 were built. Since they were produced concurrently with the MG TC, the Y-Types used the same XPAG engines, with the same modifications.

YB

The YB, introduced in 1951, improved on one of the YA's faults, its brakes. Up front were two leading shoes on the drum brakes that would help the YB stop more quickly. Also, the YB had a front sway bar, which reduced the tendency to oversteer, as well as smaller wheels. Larger shock absorbers were fitted to the rear wheels and the rear axle was changed to a hypoid design, matching that on the TD. A heater was finally offered as an optional extra.

Neither the YA nor YB was intended for export. It wasn't until the introduction of the Z Magnette that any consideration was given to exporting an MG sedan.

Y-Type Restoration

Rust is always a problem with all-steel chassis, and the Y-Types were particularly prone to rust at the rear end. The rear body mountings can corrode and the trunk can be heard banging against the body when the car is in motion. The spare tire well is the best place to check for any rust of the rear body mountings.

Body mounting bolts are also located inside the car under the carpeting in front of

Powering the Y-Type was a single carburetor version of the 1,250-cc "TC" engine. With the single carb the engine developed only 46 brake horsepower versus 54.4 brake horsepower in the TC. Since the Y-Type weighed 550 pounds more than the TC, its performance suffered. One advantage, though, was that the engine could be tuned to full TC specifications, which made speeds of over 100 miles per hour possible. *Margaret Harrison*

Instrumentation was fairly basic in the Y-Type, with a speedometer and accessory gauges, no tachometer. However, the gauges were set in octagonal bezels in a wood dash that gave an air of elegance to the car. *Margaret Harrison*

the rear seats. You should also check around the inside of the rear wheel arches for rust, because the sunroof drains exit at this location. Another rust area is the bottom of the bulkhead area in front. The front suspension is usually reliable if it has been well maintained. At this time in the car's life, though, regular maintenance is to be expected, unless you find a "sleeper" in a barn somewhere. It's the same with the rack-and-pinion steering. Replacement kits may still be available for the brakes, which in the YB, at least, were the same as the TD.

The drivetrain is the same as used on the MG TD, and spares should be available. The engine is noted for leaking oil, but if oil pressure is between 40 and 70 psi at 40 miles per hour, the engine is okay. Check to see if the oil filter is the throwaway type, which was installed after engine No. XPAG/SC 15405. The gearbox is identical to the TD/TF and is fragile. Check for noise and abuse. In the rear, the YA's axle does use up half shafts. The YB, with a hypoid rear axle, is more reliable.

Parts for the Y-Type, other than body panels, are as available as those of the TD, on which it was based. In this case, engine, transmission, and suspension parts may be found through any MG TD source, either as used or aftermarket parts. Body panels are exceptionally rare in the United States, since the cars weren't imported, although it should be easier to find these parts in Britain.

Magnette, Type ZA, ZB

The "Z" Magnette was considered by many to be one of the handsomest sedans of its time. It broke away from all previous MG sedan styling, while its taut and precise handling characteristics endeared it to enthusiasts.

The "Z" was the first MG sedan to be designed under the aegis of BMC. It was announced at the 1953 London Motor Show. The MG's body was essentially that of the Wolseley 4/44, which had been announced a year earlier, but it sported an "MG"-type grille that changed its character entirely. Oddly, the Wolseley used an MG engine, while the MG Magnette used a completely new engine, one developed by BMC.

The ZA, introduced in 1952 (1954 version shown), was a version of the BMC Wolsley 4/44 with a 1,489-cc engine and a faux MG grille. This was the same engine as was used in the MGA, although in the ZA it developed only 60 horsepower. In the later ZB, larger carburetors were fitted that increased horsepower to the 68 of the MGA.

Named after the first Magnette, the K1/KA, which was also a sedan, the Z-Type was the first MG of monocoque construction. Yet it was taut and sturdy and outperformed the 1 1/2-liter Y-Type in every way. It was also roomier and more comfortable than its predecessor, with better acceleration, a higher top speed, and improved handling. The front suspension was independent by coil springs and double unequal wishbones. The shock absorber was telescopic and enclosed by the spring. In the rear, the semielliptic springs were used with a live axle, with telescopic shock absorbers. Inside, there was plenty of wood, with a veneer dash surrounding the instruments; it had no tachometer.

The ZA had no components that were interchangeable with any other MG model.

Essentially identical to the ZA, except for the flashing on the front fender, the ZB also offered the larger carburetors on the 1,489-cc engine, giving the car 68 horsepower. Bolt-on disc wheels were used, as with the sports car, and the ZA/ZB used four-wheel drum brakes.

One option for the Z-Magnette was a two-tone paint scheme, mimicking those used in the United States. Actually, the two-tone scheme gave a little panache to a fairly dull sedan. The Varitone models are very rare. More than 35,000 Z-Magnettes were produced between 1953 and 1958. *Margaret Harrison*

Rather, it was the forerunner of modern production techniques, and was actually ahead of the sports car design. The heater was standard. In 1956, the ZA was superseded by the ZB, with a considerable increase in power, gained by increasing the compression ratio, fitting larger carburetors and double valve springs. Among the few body changes were the addition of a full-width parcel shelf in the ZB, one way to tell them apart, and a dished steering wheel. A ZB Varitone model was introduced, with a wraparound rear windshield.

In 1958, a two-tone "Varitone" model was introduced. The ZB also used a form of automatic transmission called Manumatic. It used a conventional clutch, which was operated hydraulically by the engine inlet manifold vacuum, engine speed, and a switch on the gear lever.

Classic Cars magazine recently rated twenty British sports sedans. Of the Z-Type Magnette, they wrote, "Jelly-mould [styling] it may be but it's probably the cleanest, simplest design of the lot [which included a Bentley Continental R, Jowett Javelin, Riley RM, and Sunbeam Talbot 90]. Unfortunately, the dashboard smacks of indecision within the Abingdon styling department. Standard instrumentation peeps through cut-outs in the wood on either side of the speedometer, which are underlined by octagon-shaped switches and knobs, but there's a nod toward modernity in the form of a roof-mounted clock.

"The MG is cheap, has good performance for the size of engine, and plenty of room. Invest in plenty of sound-deadening equipment and you could be touring in a car that catches the eye and is a practical daily driver."

Magnette Mark III

The Mark III was introduced in 1959 to a less than enthusiastic reception from MG fans. No longer designed or built by MG, the Mark III had a Pininfarina design that had a wider vertical bar grille, square profile, tall vertical taillights, and fins on the rear fenders. The new Magnette was almost identical to the Morris Oxford, and differed from the Austin and Wolseley sedans in the grille and trim details. It offered leather-upholstered bucket seats up front with walnut interior trim. The engine was the 1,489-cc BMC "B" engine. Wheels were 14-inch diameter, but performance was sluggish. The Mark III had wood trim inside and an MG-like grille, as well as a double carburetor version of the MGA 1,588-cc engine.

Magnette Mark IV

Everything was bigger in the Mark IV, introduced in 1961, compared with the Mark III. The engine was the 1,622-cc version from the MGA 1600 Mark II, the wheelbase was an inch longer, and an automatic transmission was now available. The suspension and steering geometry were improved, as was the body, which made it able to handle the highways at a brisk rate of speed. The Mark IV continued until 1968, when it was dropped.

MG 1100

Selling concurrently with the Mark IV was the new MG 1100. Again, this car was not designed by MG but by BMC resident genius Alec Issigonis, father of the Mini. The BMC 1100-based sedans were the top selling cars in Britain for many years. Over 3 million

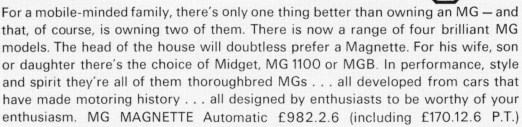

WHAT'S TWICE AS GOOD AS OWNING AN MG

For a mobile-minded family, there's only one thing better than owning an MG — and that, of course, is owning two of them. There is now a range of four brilliant MG models. The head of the house will doubtless prefer a Magnette. For his wife, son or daughter there's the choice of Midget, MG 1100 or MGB. In performance, style and spirit they're all of them thoroughbred MGs . . . all developed from cars that have made motoring history . . . all designed by enthusiasts to be worthy of your enthusiasm. MG MAGNETTE Automatic £982.2.6 (including £170.12.6 P.T.) Manual gearbox £899.19.2(including £156.9.2 P.T.). MG MIDGET £623.17.1 (including £108.17.1 P.T.). Also **MG 1100** £742.5.5 (inc £129.5.5 P.T.). **MGB** £855.5.0 (inc £148.15.0 P.T.).

Safety fast!

THE **BRITISH** MOTOR CORPORATION LTD
Backed by 12 Months' Warranty and B.M.C. Service—
Express, Expert, Everywhere.

THE M.G. CAR CO. LTD., SALES DIVISION, LONGBRIDGE, BIRMINGHAM. OVERSEAS BUSINESS: B.M.C. EXPORT SALES LIMITED, BIRMINGHAM & PICCADILLY W.1.

MG continued the Magnette name with the Mark III, introduced in 1959. Here was a true "badge engineered" car that was identical to the Morris Oxford except for the grille. The car used the same 1,489-cc engine as the Z-Magnette and the original MGA, which had now moved on to a 1,588-cc unit.

1100/1300 cars were sold between 1962 and 1973. The MG versions were the most popular. The 1100 was revolutionary, and was described in promotional literature as "the most advanced MG of all time." It was launched at the same time as the MGB, and was overshadowed by the new sports car.

Originally, there were plans to introduce an MG version of the Mini that was introduced in 1959. However, after John Cooper's cars won the world manufacturer's championship twice, the Cooper name was attached to the hot Mini, with Austin and Morris versions of the car produced. This canceled any plans for an MG version.

Various MG-badged design exercises were penned for the Mini, including two-seater versions, but Issigonis put the kibosh

Instrumentation in the Magnette made it clear the car was not an MG. Instead of a full array of instruments, the driver had only a large speedometer and four accessory gauges—any "proper" sports car would have had a tachometer. Luxury, instead, was the watchword, with a walnut dash and locking glove box.

on these because he felt the front-wheel design was not ideal for a sports car. But BMC wanted a small sedan to market alongside the Mark III and Mark IV Magnettes. Therefore, the MG 1100 was launched about a year after the Austin and Morris versions. It received a lukewarm welcome but was a

Front seats are of the smooth-action, fully adjusting bucket type. Rear seat has fold-back central arm-rest and door-pull side-rests. Cushions are full Latex foam, and upholstery is in fine-quality English leather on all wearing parts.

Inside the Magnette Mark III was seating for four in relative comfort, with a fold-down arm rest for the rear seat passengers. Leather facing was used on all the seats, adding to the MG image.

Successor to the Mark III was the Mark IV Magnette, with the 1,622-cc engine of the MGA 1600 Mark II, but delivering only 68 brake horsepower. An automatic transmission was available on the car. There were 15,676 Mark II models sold over a two-year period, but a mere 13,738 Mark IVs sold over seven years.

British Motor Industry Heritage Trust

good seller. Sales were about 28,000 over the first five years.

The 1100 retained the same transverse front engine and front-wheel drive as the popular Mini, and used the 1,098-cc engine in twin-carburetor form. It was closely related to similar Austin, Morris, and Vanden Plas 1100 models. The engine developed 55 horsepower at 5,500 rpm, and could pull the car along at 88 miles per hour.

The unibody car was available first in two-door, but a four-door version was offered later. It was felt the two-door version was more in keeping with MG's sporting image. And the two-door was designed to compete with the prime imported car in the American market, the Volkswagen Beetle. This was the first MG with front-wheel drive, Hydrolastic four-wheel independent suspension that used wishbone-type control arms in front and trailing arms in the rear, but there were no conventional springs or shock absorbers. Instead, hermetically sealed rubber barrels contained a special liquid, and the units at the front and rear were connected to produce a common supply of fluid. The Hydrolastic suspension provided exceptional ride characteristics.

The new suspension eliminated pitching movements because the front and rear suspensions were interconnected.

Styling touches included a slim windshield frame and door pillars with curved side glass. The grille was similar to that on the Mark IV Magnette, with multiple vertical bars split into two sections by a vertical bar. Front bucket seats and front disc brakes were standard. The MG 1100 was capable of carrying four adults, where the Mini was cramped.

In the 1964 model year, a more luxurious Princess model joined the 1100 lineup. The Princess had coachbuilt bodywork and a plush interior with a walnut dash and folding picnic tables.

When BMC/MG installed the 1275 Mini Cooper engine in the MG 1100, it was renamed the MG 1300. For a while, there was a market in Chile for fiberglass models of this car. In any case, the larger engine gave the MG 1300 much sportier performance. *Margaret Harrison*

Another badge-engineered BMC car, the MG 1100, used a 1,098-cc engine mounted transversely in a front-wheel drive chassis. The suspension was the unique element of this vehicle, as it used hydraulics to act as shock absorbers and keep the car level. The later MG 1300 used the same 1,275-cc engine that made the Mini Cooper such a pocket rocket. *Plain English Archive*

With its 1,098-cc engine, the MG1100 Sports Sedan was not noted for its outstanding performance. However, handling was unique for a small car because of the unique hydrolastic suspension. The 1100 was a badge-engineered version of similar Austin and Morris front-wheel drive sedans. *British Motor Industry Heritage Trust*

THIS NEEDLE MOVES FROM LEFT TO RIGHT... IN SECONDS

THIS NEEDLE HARDLY MOVES AT ALL ...FOR MILES

The MG "Sports Sedan" was another name variation of the MG 1100 and 1300, but in fact it was the same car. The MG 1100 was bigger than the Minis that were so popular in Europe and provides greater creature comforts for the passengers.

MG in the United States advertised the MG1100 (or Sports Sedan) as part sedan, part sports car. The company used then Grand Prix Champion Graham Hill, a man with a dual personality of his own, to promote the car in this ad.

One of the biggest club sporting events of the 1960s and 1970s was the Long Island MG Car Club's 1,000-mile rally. MG took advantage of the popularity of this event to advertise the MG 1100, or Sports Sedan. Here was an event where the little MG could shine, as Time-Speed-Distance rallying, at least as practiced in the United States, was more of a precision driving event than one that called for all-out speed.

The 1100 (or rather the suspension) was the basis behind an entry in the Indianapolis 500 by Kjell Qvale, BMC's West Coast distributor. Qvale built three rear-engined Offenhauser cars for the race, with a Hydrolastic-type suspension system. A. J. Foyt was scheduled to drive one of the "MG Liquid Suspension Specials," but changed his mind, switched to a then-conventional front-engined car, and won the 1964 race. Pedro Rodriguez crashed one of the cars in practice and didn't start. Bob Vieth started and didn't finish. Walt Hansgen drove the third car and, despite spending 27 minutes in the pits with a faulty fuel pump, finished

12th and last. In 1965, the three MG Specials were driven by Hansgen, Vieth, and Jerry Grant, but none of them finished.

MG 1300

In 1968, MG introduced the MG 1300, which was the 1100 front-wheel drive sedan with a 1,275-cc engine. The car not only gained a slight increase in power, it also gained a new personality. Where the 1100 was uncomfortable cruising at speeds over 70 miles per hour (we're talking about in Europe), the 1300 could reach 90 on the speedometer and spend all day cruising at

Please don't drink the suspension system...

Not good for you: we had to add dye to the alcohol-and-water mix in order to avoid paying a liquor tax on every MG Sports Sedan we import.

Besides, there are greater kicks to be had from our new Hydrolastic® Suspension. Teamed with front wheel drive, it gives our five-passenger economy sedan the handling qualities of an expensive sports car. Permanently sealed in fluid replaces metal springs and shock absorbers. You corner flat, ride level and hold firm to the road. Most intoxicating, whether you motor for fun or family.

The Sports Sedan earns its name in other ways, as well. MG's 1100 c.c. twin-carburetor power plant hastens you on your way. The big fade free disc brakes impose control seldom experienced off the race course. The bucket seats and 4-speed stick shift add to the sport.

And it's all yours at a price usually referred to as laughably low.

Want a drink? See your favorite bartender.

Want the sporting life in a family car? See your MG dealer.

In either case . . . cheers.

FOR OVERSEAS DELIVERY AND OTHER INFORMATION, WRITE: THE BRITISH MOTOR CORP./HAMBRO, INC., DEPT. SF, 734 GRAND AVENUE, RIDGEFIELD, NEW JERSEY

With the 1,275-cc engine of the all-conquering Mini-Cooper, the MG1300 had a top speed of over 90 mph and could run all day at speeds near 75 mph. The interior was more luxurious, as can be seen in this right-hand drive version, with a walnut-trimmed dash and instrument cluster similar to that found in a Jaguar sedan.

75. The top speed also benefitted from a new final drive ratio of 3.65:1, which gave 17.1 miles per hour per 1,000 rpm in top gear versus 14.9 miles per hour per 1,000 rpm in top for the 1100.

Concurrent with the new engine, MG (BMC) also introduced new seats, wipers, lights, and an all-synchromesh gearbox for manual-transmission cars. An automatic transmission was offered as an option with a single SU carburetor. The engine developed 70 horsepower, and the dash and instruments were improved. The four-door version of the 1300 was dropped in 1969, as was the automatic transmission. The entire line was removed from the MG line in 1971, as British Leyland put its emphasis behind the Austin GT.

Also in 1968, on May 14 to be precise, British Motor Holdings and the Leyland Motor Corporation, manufacturers of Triumph sports cars among others, merged to form the British Leyland Motor Corporation. It was the biggest merger of two companies in England's history. The new firm combined MG, Standard Triumph, Austin-Healey, Daimler, Rover, Austin, Coventry Climax, Morris, Wolseley, Riley, and Jaguar into one company, comprising about 85 percent of Britain's motor industry.

The hydrolastic suspension of the MG 1100 and 1300 sedans was an alcohol-and-water mixture that connected the suspensions of all four wheels. When one wheel went over a bump, fluid would be transferred to the other wheels, keeping the car level.

SPECIFICATIONS

YA/YB/YT

Production dates: 4/47–12/51 (YA/YT); 12/51–8/53 (YB)

Total production: 6,158 (YA); 1,301 (YB); 877 (YT)

Chassis numbers: 4.0251-4.7285; YB.025-YB.1551

Engine numbers: (YA) XPAG/SC/10001–XPAG/SC/16915, XPAG/SC/2/16916–XPAG/SC/2/17462; (YT) XPAG/T/; (YB) XPAG/SC/2/16916–XPAG/SC/2/17462; XPAG/SC2/17463–XPAG/SC2/18460

Price: $2,658 POE (YA); $2,875 POE (YT)

Engine:

    Type: Four cylinder cast iron pushrod operated overhead valves

    Displacement: 1,250 cc

    Bore: 66.5 mm

    Stroke: 90 mm

    Compression ratio: 7.3 to 7.5:1

    BHP: 46 @ 4,800 rpm; 54 @ 5,400 rpm (YT)

    Torque: 64 ft-lbs @ 2,600 rpm

    Red line: 5,700 rpm

Transmission:

    Type: Four-speed manual with synchromesh on top three gears

    Clutch: Single plate dry clutch 7-1/4 in

    Overall gear ratios:

        4th*   1.00:1

        3rd*   1.39:1

        2nd*   2.07:1

        1st   3.50:1

        Reverse 3.50:1

        *Synchromesh

    Rear axle ratio: 5.143:1 (YA/YT); 5.125:1 (YB)

Chassis

    Type: Box section steel with tie-rod bracing to firewall structure.

    Wheels: Bolt-on pressed steel 3x16 in (YA/YT); 4Jx15 (YB)

    Tires: 5.25x16 (YA/YT); 5.50x15 (YB)

    Brakes: Lockheed hydraulic 9-in drums (YB had two leading shoes in front)

    Steering: Rack and pinion

    Front suspension: Independent by coil spring and wishbone. Luvax-Girling hydraulic shock absorbers. YB added anti-roll bar

    Rear suspension: Underslung by semielliptic leaf springs, Panhard rod at rear. Luvax-Girling hydraulic shock absorbers

    Fuel system: Single SU carburetor, 1 1/4-in diameter (two on YT)

    Fuel tank: 8 gal

    Dimensions:

        Wheelbase: 99.0 in

        Overall length: 161.2 in (YA); 164 in (YT/YB)

        Track front: 47.375 in

        Track rear: 50 in

        Width: 59.0 in

        Height: 57.0 in

        Curb weight: 2,280 lbs (YA); 2,137 lbs (YT); 2,337 lbs (YB)

YA Driver's Handbook factory part number: AKD620
YA Parts List factory part number: AKD638
YB Driver's Handbook factory part number: AKD621
YB Workshop Manual factory part number: AKD632A
YB Parts List factory part number: AKD832

ZA/ZB

Production dates: 10/53–9/56 (ZA); 9/56–12/58 (ZB)
Total production: 12,754 (ZA); 23,846 (ZB)
Chassis numbers: 501-18,576 (ZA); 18,577-37,101 (ZB)
Engine numbers: 15GA:101-17700 approx (ZA);15GC:101-19101 approx (ZB)
Price: $2,595 POE (ZA); $2,535 POE (ZB)
Engine:

    Type: Cast iron four cylinder with pushrod overhead valves
    Displacement: 1,489 cc
    Bore: 73.025 mm
    Stroke: 89 mm
    Compression ratio: 7.15:1 (ZA); 8.3:1 (ZB)
    BHP: 60 @ 4,600 rpm (ZA); 68 @ 5,250 rpm (ZB)
    Torque: 78.3 ft-lbs @ 3,000 rpm (ZA); 83 ft-lbs @ 3,500 rpm
    Red line: 5,800 rpm

Transmission

    Type: Four-speed gearbox with synchromesh on top three gears
    Clutch: Single-plate dry clutch
    Overall gear ratios:

4th	1.00:1
3rd	1.374:1
2nd	2.214:1
1st	3.64:1
Reverse	4.76:1

    Rear axle ratio: 4.875:1 (ZA); 4.55:1 (ZB)

Chassis:

    Type: Monocoque, welded steel
    Wheels: Bolt-on pressed steel, 4Jx15
    Tires: 5.50x15
    Brakes: Lockheed hydraulic with 10-in drums, two leading shoes at front
    Steering: Cam Gears rack and pinion
    Front suspension: Independent by coil springs and wishbones. Telescopic hydraulic shock absorbers
    Rear suspension: Nonindependent by semielliptic leaf springs. Telescopic hydraulic shock absorbers
    Fuel system: Twin 1-1/4 in SU semidowndraft carburetors ZA, type H2; ZB 1-in type H4
    Fuel tank: 9.25 gal
    Dimensions:

        Wheelbase: 102.0 in
        Overall length: 169.0 in
        Track front: 51.0 in
        Track rear: 51.0 in
        Width: 63.0 in
        Height: 58.0 in
        Curb weight: 2,464 lbs
    Colors:
        Exterior and Interior

ZA and ZB standard

MG Green with Biscuit or Green trim; Twilight Grey with Grey Maroon trim (also on ZB); Maroon, Autumn Red with Biscuit or Maroon trim; Black with Biscuit, Maroon, Green or Grey trim (also on ZB); Steel Blue with Maroon or Black trim (also on ZB); Royal Tan with Grey trim; Island Green with Green or Black trim (also on ZB); Birch Grey with Maroon or Grey trim (also on ZB); Damask Red with Maroon or Biscuit trim (also on ZB).

ZB Varitone

Birch Grey/Twilight Grey
Ivory/Autumn Red
Island Green/Sage Green
Steel Blue/Mineral Blue
Ivory/Black
Birch Grey/Black
Island Green/Black
Island Green/Reseda Green
Steel Blue/Black
Island Green/Dark Green
Kashmir Beige/Wolseley Maroon

ZA Driver's Handbook factory part number: AKD572E
ZA Workshop Manual factory part number: AKD573A
ZA Parts List factory part number: AKD688
ZB Driver's Handbook factory part number: AKD687L
ZB Workshop Manual factory part number: AKD573A
ZB Parts List factory part number: AKD688

Mk III

Production dates: Early 1959–late 1961
Total production: 15,676
Price: $2,695 POE
Engine:

Type: Cast iron inline four with overhead valves
Displacement: 1,489 cc
Bore: 73.025 mm
Stroke: 88.9 mm
Compression ratio: 8.3:1
BHP: 66.5 @ 5,200 rpm
Torque: 85 ft-lbs @ 3,300 rpm
Red line: 5,500 rpm

Transmission

Type: Four-speed manual
Clutch: Dry clutch
Overall gear ratios:

4th	4.3:1
3rd	5.91:1
2nd	9.52:1
1st	15.64:1
Reverse	20.45:1

Rear axle ratio: 4.3:1

Chassis:

Type: Unibody
Wheels: Bolt-on discs
Tires: 5.60x14
Brakes: Girling hydraulic 9-in drums, two leading shoes in front
Steering: Rack and pinion
Front suspension: Coil and wishbone
Rear suspension: Semielliptic leaf springs
Fuel system: Two semidowndraft SU carburetors
Fuel tank: 12 gal
Dimensions:
       Wheelbase: 99.2 in
       Overall length: 178.0 in
       Track front: 48.6 in
       Track rear: 49.9 in
       Width: 63.5 in
       Height: 59.8 in
       Ground clearance: 6.5 in
       Curb weight: 2,492 lbs
Driver's Handbook factory part number: AKD1028F
Workshop Manual factory part number: AKD1027C
Parts List factory part number: AKD953

Mk IV
Production dates: Late 1961–early 1968
Total production: 13,738
Price: $2,695 POE
Engine:
       Type: Cast iron inline four
       Displacement: 1,622 cc
       Bore: 76.2 mm
       Stroke: 88.9 mm
       Compression ratio: 8.3:1
       BHP: 68 @ 5,000 rpm
       Torque: 83 ft-lbs @ 3,000 rpm
       Red line: 5,500 rpm
Transmission:
       Type: Four-speed manual, automatic available
       Clutch: Dry clutch
       Overall gear ratios:
            4th   N/A
            3rd   N/A
            2nd   N/A
            1st   N/A
            Reverse N/A
       Rear axle ratio: 4.30:1
Chassis:
       Type: Front engine rear drive
       Wheels: Bolt-on discs
       Tires: 5.60x14
       Brakes: Girling hydraulic 9-in drums, two leading shoes in front

Steering: Cam and lever
Front suspension: Coil and wishbone with anti-roll bar
Rear suspension: Semielliptic leaf springs with stabilizer
Fuel system: Two semidowndraft SU carburetors
Fuel tank: 12 gal
Dimensions:

      Wheelbase: 100.25 in
      Overall length: 178.0 in
      Track front: 50.6 in
      Track rear: 51.4 in
      Width: 63.5 in
      Height: 59.8 in

Driver's Handbook factory part number: AKD1028F
Workshop Manual factory part number: AKD1027C
Parts List factory part number: AKD953

MG1100

Production dates: Late 1962–mid-1971
Total production: 116,827
Price: $1,898 POE (two-door); $2,169 POE (four-door); $3,016 (Princess)
Engine:

      Type: Transverse cast iron inline four
      Displacement: 1,098 cc
      Bore: 64.58 mm
      Stroke: 83.72 mm
      Compression ratio: 8.9:1
      BHP: 55 @ 5,500 rpm
      Torque: 61 ft-lbs @2,500 rpm
      Red line: 5,500rpm

Transmission:

      Type: Four-speed manual
      Clutch: 7 1/2-in BMC single dry plate
      Overall gear ratios:

            4th   4.13:1
            3rd   5.83:1
            2nd   8.98:1
            1st   14.99:1
            Reverse 14.99:1

      Final drive ratio: 4.13:1

Chassis:

      Type: Monocoque steel with transverse engine, front wheel drive
      Wheels:Bolt-on discs
      Tires: 5.50x12
      Brakes: Front disc, rear drum
      Steering: Rack and pinion
      Front suspension: Hydrolastic with wishbones
      Rear suspension: Hydrolastic with trailing arms and anti-roll bar
      Fuel system: Two semidowndraft SU
      Fuel tank: 10 gal

      Dimensions:
            Wheelbase: 93.5 in

Overall length: 146.75 in
Track front: 51.5 in
Track rear: 50.9 in
Width: 60.0 in
Height: 52.75 in
Curb weight: 1,806 lbs

Driver's Handbook factory part number: AKD3287B
Workshop Manual factory part number: AKD3294A
Parts List factory part number: AKD3008 For two-door models, supplemental part number AKD3421 applies

MG 1300

Production dates: 1968–1971
Total production: 26,240
Price: $2,250
Engine:
      Type: Transverse cast iron inline four
      Displacement: 1,275 cc
      Bore: 70.63 mm
      Stroke: 81.33 mm
      Compression ratio: 8.8:1
      BHP: 65 @ 6,000 rpm
      Torque: 72 ft-lbs @ 3,000 rpm
      Red line: 6,500 rpm
Transmission:
      Type: Front drive, four-speed manual, automatic optional
      Clutch: Dry
      Overall gear ratios:

4th	4.13:1
3rd	5.83:1
2nd	8.98:1
1st	14.99:1
Reverse	14.99:1

      Final drive ratio: 3.65:1
Chassis:
      Type: two-door and four-door sedans
      Wheels: Bolt-on discs
      Tires: 5.50x12
      Brakes: Lockheed discs front, drums rear
      Steering: Rack and pinion
      Front suspension: Hydrolastic fluid filled
      Rear suspension: Hydrolastic fluid filled
      Fuel system: Single downdraft SU
      Fuel tank: 10 gal
      Dimensions:
            Wheelbase: 93.5 in
            Overall length: 146.75 in
            Track front: 51.5 in
            Track rear: 50.9 in
            Width: 60.5 in
            Height: 52.0 in
            Curb weight: 1,880 lbs

Chapter 7

MGS After 1981

Sedans

After MG ceased production at Abingdon in 1981, a few attempts were made to keep the name alive. All the ensuing cars were built in Longbridge, as Abingdon was closed down.

First of these was a sedan called the MG Metro, a badge-engineered version of the Austin/Morris Mini, using the 1,275-cc Mini engine. Mike Allison, in *MG: The Magic of the Marque*, described the MG Metro 1300 thusly: "A nice exterior finish was specified, and alloy wheels shod with a low-profile tire were featured, all of which distinguished the car from its cheaper stablemates. If the gearbox ratios were not ideal, at least the car could be hustled along in a way to give joy to any true MG driver. Kimber might not have approved of the cheap plastic interior and stylized instruments, but all the flair of a contemporary-designed sporty car was present."

Bill Boddy in *Motor Sport* said the Metro was much more civilized than the Mini, which was great praise indeed. The Metro's engine had a higher compression ratio (10.5:1 versus 9.71:1) than the Mini, but used only one SU carburetor for a final output of 72 horsepower at 6,000 rpm versus the Mini's 75 horsepower at 5,800 rpm. The other major change from the Mini was that the Metro used cast aluminum wheels with low-profile tires and a rear spoiler. Inside there were rally-style seats and a small diameter padded steering wheel, which were designed to appeal to enthusiasts. The Metro used a Hydragas suspension system that was similar to the Hydrolastic suspension of the MG 1100/1300.

The MG Metro was a good seller, with 38,635 sales in its first two years. In 1982, the MG Metro Turbo was announced, with an exhaust-driven turbocharger adding boost. Beside the turbo, the crankshaft was nitrided,

After MG ceased producing sports cars, the company formed from the ashes of British Leyland, Austin Rover, built the MG Metro 1300, which was a badge- engineered version of the Mini, using the same 1,275-cc engine. The Metro used a Hydragas suspension system that was similar to the Hydrolastic suspension of the MG1100/1300. *British Motor Industry Heritage Trust*

the pistons and lower-end bearings were stronger, and there was a bigger oil pump and an oil cooler. For cooling there was an improved radiator and bigger water passages in the head, as well as sodium-cooled exhaust valves and double valve springs. The suspension was stiffer with better springs, and a rear antiroll bar joined a thicker front one. Wider wheels and 60-series tires gave the car a lower profile, while a deeper front air dam offered better aerodynamics.

The engine was rated at a robust 93 horsepower at 6,150 rpm. Unfortunately, the car was hampered by the lack of a five-speed gearbox. (The Issigonis "gearbox in the sump" transmission had poor accessibility and a cramped layout that prevented the addition of a fifth gear.) Examples of the MG Metro can be bought cheaply in Britain, but the cars were never legally imported into the United States. It has the A-plus engine, which is reliable.

Major controls should be easy to use. If there is shuddering in the clutch, it may need repair or replacement. This, combined with a shaking engine, will put strain on the exhaust headers and may cause a fracture. The engine tends to be noisy. Any wear in the idler gear, which shares the sump with the engine, can cause a knocking sound when the engine is revved. Check the exhaust for excessive smoke. The water hose from the inlet manifold to the radiator tends to rub on the engine mounting. Also, the electric fan does not operate until the engine is about 3/4 hot.

A sagging suspension is a sign that the pressure in the Hydragas suspension has leaked. Aluminum wheels are pretty, but they suffer from damage and corrosion. The front wheels may also have too much play, which can be detected by pulling them at the top. As with all British cars, bodywork is subject to rust, especially on the front fenders behind the headlights and inside the fender in front of the door pillar. Steel bumpers can also rust, and the front fascia can develop rust pockets if it has been subjected to stone chipping. The same malady can affect the rear wheel arches and the front ends of the sills. Check the bottoms of the doors for rust damage, too.

MG Metro Turbo. *British Motor Industry Heritage Trust*

MG Maestro

Next in the line of MG sedans was the MG Maestro 1600, introduced in 1983, with a more powerful engine and a five-speed manual gearbox. The Maestro, designed with British Leyland's CAD/CAM design system, used a MacPherson strut front suspension and a trailing arm rear suspension with torsion bars and coil springs. Two engines were available, a 1,275-cc with a Volkswagen-designed five-speed gearbox and a 1,598-cc. These engines drove the front wheels in the modern idiom. The larger engine was rated at 81 horsepower in standard form, but this could be improved to 103 horsepower with dual Weber carburetors on an eight-port manifold.

The car had digital instruments, a voice synthesizer, and a powerful engine. The original engines used twin-choke Weber carburetors mounted on a short inlet manifold. The early cars suffered from excess heat in the engine compartment and were difficult to start. In July 1984, the engine was changed from the R series to the S series, which meant a change from a chain-driven camshaft to a toothed camshaft belt, a redesigned cylinder head, lightweight block/crankcase, and improvements to the water and oil pumps.

Introduced in 1982, the turbocharged version of the MG Metro had an engine that delivered 93 horsepower. The Hydragas suspension was stiffer in the Turbo, with wider, low-profile tires and a deeper front air dam that made it into a performance car. Austin Rover campaigned the Metro in several international rallies in the early 1980s. *British Motor Industry Heritage Trust*

In October 1984, a 2-liter electronic fuel injected engine was introduced, the same as used on the new Montego. The Maestro also gained ventilated front disc brakes and a rear antiroll bar. The Maestro Turbo is the ultimate Maestro, with a color-coded styling kit by Tickford. Adding the turbo increases power to about 150 horsepower, which can move it from 0 to 60 miles per hour in under seven seconds. Only 500 of these cars were built and they are very rare.

The Maestro's suspension was by MacPherson struts, with lower wishbones and an antiroll bar. The rear suspension was by struts as well. There can be wear in the suspension bushings and shock absorbers that will ruin the handling. The five-speed gearbox is the same as that used in the Volkswagen Golf. Corrosion is a problem with Maestros. Check along the lower sections of the doors, inside the front wheel arches, and around the inside and outside of the rear fenders.

Metro Turbo as rally competitor. *British Motor Industry Heritage Trust*

MG Montego

Where the Maestro was a hatchback, in U.S. terminology, the next in the line, the MG Montego, with a 2-liter S-series engine, had conventional "three-box styling" with a proper trunk. The 1994 fuel injected O-series engine was mated to a Honda-designed five-speed manual transmission.

In turbocharged form, the MG Montego Turbo proved to be the fastest production MG of all time, and could still carry four adults. The Montego used the same floor pan as the Maestro, but had a wheelbase that was 10 inches longer. The car was 16 inches longer than the Maestro and offered more than 18 cubic feet of luggage space. Three engines were available: the faithful 1,275, the 1,598-cc, and a new 2-liter design. The 2-liter engine, with Lucas fuel injection, could produce 115 horsepower at 5,500 rpm. The Montego Turbo was introduced in August 1985, with power up to 150 horsepower. The Montego was a popular fleet car in Britain, so any prospective buyer should check for excessive mileage or wear.

MG competed in international rallies with a mid-engined V6 version of the Metro, the MG Metro Turbo 6R4 (six-cylinder, Rally car, four-wheel drive), a spoiler over the back end, and wide tires. While it was available in England on a limited basis, it and the other post-MG MGs never reached the United States. The all-aluminum 2-liter V6 was rated at 240 horsepower.

Sports Cars—RV-8 and MGF

In 1983, a organization known as the British Motor Industry Heritage Trust was formed to honor the British motor industry. The Trust had a cash-generating arm, British Motor Heritage, headed by Peter Mitchell. BMH was a parts and approval arm of BMIHT, with 75 percent of its profits directed toward support of the parent. In 1984, David Bishop joined the Heritage organization as assistant managing director. Bishop had worked for Pressed Steel Fisher and had 23 years of body manufacturing experience behind him. He began, in 1987, to track down the pressing tools and jigs for the MGB, all of which were still in a former Pressed Steel factory.

Successor to the Metro was the Maestro, with a 1,600-cc engine that developed 83 horsepower in standard trim and 103 horsepower when fitted with twin Weber carburetors. This front-wheel drive sedan also used MacPherson strut suspension. *British Motor Industry Heritage Trust*

A factory was occupied in Faringdon and MGB bodies were built there. Originally intended as replacement bodies for MGBs, the first was finished on February 20, 1988. This was a pre-1975 chrome-bumper version, right-hand drive. A left-hand-drive version was completed in 1990, after which a short run of MGB/GT bodies was built, as were some "rubber baby buggy bumper" roadsters. After this, BMH began building MG Midget bodies, and followed with TR6 bodies.

After building bodies, and proving that it could be successful at it, BMH decided to build a complete car. A Rover 3.9-liter V-8 was secured and installed in a left-hand drive roadster. When testing proved that such a project was worthwhile, the MG RV-8 was authorized. Original plans called for a build of no more than 15 per week, for a total build of around 2,000. A new badge was designed to commemorate the car. The MGA's badge through its life was a chocolate MG monogram set against a cream octagonal background. The MGB's badge had chrome lettering and a red background. The RV-8's MG badge reverted back to the chocolate-and-cream badge of the MGA.

In 1995, Rover announced a true new MG, the MGF. Here was a totally new car,

The last MG sedan under Austin Rover management was the Montego, with a 2.0-liter engine. Unlike the hatchback sedans which had preceded it, the Montego was a conventional "three box" design with a decent trunk. In 1994, the engine was changed to the O-series unit. In turbocharged form, it became the fastest production MG ever made. *British Motor Industry Heritage Trust*

powered by a mid-mounted 1,796-cc 16-valve four-cylinder engine from Rover's K series. In its mildest form, the MGF 1.8i delivers 120 horsepower at 5,500 rpm. With variable valve control, the MGF 1.8iVVC is rated at 145 horsepower at 7,000 rpm.

Rover's version of variable valve control differs from Honda's VTEC system. Rover varies the point at which the inlet valves

The MGF is very much in the modern idiom, but it is still an MG. It wears the MG octagon in the center of its grille and presents a face to the public not unlike that of the later MGBs. But it is powered by a 1.8-liter, 16-valve four-cylinder Rover "K" engine, mounted transversely behind the passenger compartment.

open and close and the time they remain open during each camshaft revolution. Eccentric drives enable each of the four cams to vary their angle anywhere between 220 and 295 degrees. The advantage is greater combustion control.

On the road, the engine is crisp and smooth. According to Rover, the 0–60 mile per hour time of the 1.8iVVC is 7.0 seconds, and the top speed is in the neighborhood of 130 miles per hour. On the 1.8i, 0–60 comes in 8.5 seconds and the top speed is 120 miles per hour.

Front and rear suspensions are by double wishbones with tuned compliance steering characteristics and a high-ratio steering rack. And in a link back to the MG 1100/1300 sedans, the MGF uses interconnected Hydragas units as a springing mechanism.

Inside, the car has dual airbags and the standard complement of safety features, including a pedal box to protect the driver and passenger's feet. There is more than adequate room in the cockpit, and even the tallest drivers can find adequate legroom. Instruments are black on white. Creature comforts include power windows, a competent HVAC system, electric clock, and an oil temperature gauge.

In the area of styling, the MGF is an MG from the front, if only because of the split grille and MG octagon badge in the center. In the rear, the MGF has a hint of the 1985 MG EXE dream car.

The MGF was priced at around $25,600 for the 1.8i and $30,000 for the VVC version at its introduction. Reports from England are that the car is selling well and has had some competition successes. It will not be sold in the United States, according to Rover.

SPECIFICATIONS

MG RV-8
Production dates: 1992-1995
Total production: N/A
Chassis numbers: MG90000251–
Engine numbers:
Price: $43,000 (est.)
Engine:
>Type: Aluminum Rover 3.9-liter V-8
>Displacement: 3,946 cc
>Bore: 94.0 mm
>Stroke: 71.12 mm
>Compression ratio: 9.35:1
>BHP: 190PS @ 4,750 rpm
>Torque: 318 Nm (235 ft-lbs) @ 3,200 rpm

Transmission:
>Type: LT77 five-speed fully synchronized
>Clutch:
>Overall gear ratios:

5th	0.79:1
4th	1.00:1
3rd	1.40:1
2nd	2.09:1
1st	3.32:1
Reverse	3.32:1

>Rear axle ratio: 3.31:1

Chassis:
>Type: Steel unibody
>Wheels: 6Jx15
>Tires: 205/65VR15
>Brakes: 10.6-in discs front, 9-in drums rear
>Steering: Rack and pinion
>Front suspension: Independent with double wishbones, coil springs and concentric telescopic shock absorbers
>Rear suspension: Tube type live axle with 3/4 floating drive shafts. Semielliptic taper-leaf springs. Telescopic shock absorbers, twin lower torque control arms and antiroll bar
>Fuel system: Lucas multipoint fuel injection
>Fuel tank: 11.2 gal
>Dimensions:
>>Wheelbase: 91.125 in
>>Overall length: 154.75 in (chrome bumper); 158.25 in (rubber bumper)
>>Track front: 49.0 in
>>Track rear: 49.25 in
>>Width: 59.94 in
>>Height: 49.96 in
>>Curb weight: 2,422 lbs

>Colors:
>>Exterior: Black, British Racing Green, Caribbean Blue, Flame Red, Le Mans Green, Old English White, Oxford Blue, Nightfire Red, White Gold, Woodcote Green
>>Interior: Stone Beige

Appendix

Clubs

MG Car Club

Any MG owner, or potential owner, must belong to an MG car club of some sort. This isn't a promotion for the club. Rather, it's an invitation to join with a group of people of similar interest who care about a car that's, at best, 15 years old or more. Where else can you commiserate with others and learn the foibles of your car, and perhaps even help educate others? It's a great way to learn pitfalls and hints. It's also a great way to have fun.

The mother of all MG Car Clubs, of course, is the original, founded in late 1930 by "a group of enthusiastic owners," according to Wilson McComb. The first honorary secretary of the club was an accountant by the name of John Thornley, who would, 21 years later, be named general manager of the company and would guide MG through the 1960s and 1970s to its merger with British Leyland.

According to Bob Vitrikas, the founding of the MG Car Club came after owner Roy Marsh ran an ad in The *Light Car & Cyclecar* in October 1930, inviting anyone interested informing an MG car club come to his house and talk about it. Five people answered the ad. One of the five was John Thornley. As the club grew, he would visit the factory every week. Eventually he hinted to Cecil Kimber that the company should either take over the club or hire him to run it. Kimber eventually hired Thornley.

McComb also notes that the Sports Car Club of America evolved from one U.S. branch of the MG Car Club shortly after World War II. And since the International Motor Sports Association (IMSA) and its successor, Professional Sports Car Racing, grew out of the SCCA, one could say that all American sports car racing is based on the MG Car Club and not be far from the truth.

In 1968, official BLMC support was withdrawn from the MG Car Club, as well as the Austin-Healey Owner's Club. Sadly, the official publication for both clubs, *Safety Fast*, was also canceled, although it has been reborn. *Safety Fast* was an excellent venue for MG (and Healey) owners to learn more about their cars and the tradition behind them. I owe a deep indebtedness to the magazine because it was the first publication to accept a piece of my writing more than 30 years ago.

Safety Fast, however, was not the first title of the publication. It began its life in May 1933 as *The MG Magazine*. In April 1935, a new magazine was called *The Sports Car*. John Thornley asked Wilson McComb to produce *Safety Fast* in 1959, and McComb was involved with the publication to the end. Since its rebirth, it has become a glossy four-color award-winning magazine. In its earlier form, it was a black-and-white magazine only.

The MG Car Club in Britain sponsors 14 registers offering assistance to owners of all MG models. The registers are the first source of reference for anyone interested in an MG, particularly an old one. American clubs have versions of these registers (e.g., The New England MG T Register), but the British registers should always be considered the first choice of reference.

There are 12 MG Car Club centers in England and more than 70 around the world. For information on the one nearest you, contact the MG Car Club Ltd., Membership Secretary, Kimber House, PO Box 251, Cemetery Road, Abingdon, Oxon OX14 1FF, England. The phone number (when dialing from the United States) is 011-44-235-555-552. Their fax number is 011-44-235-533-755.

You can get information on the MG Car Club on the Internet at http://www.mgcc.co.uk. Included is all information on the club and its various registers and local centers all over the world. We have included contact information on North American MG Car Clubs that was valid as of April 1997, but if you're interested in other locations around the world, you can find out on the Internet.

MGCC Registers

Vintage Register: For the Bullnose and Flatnose 14/28 (1924-27), the Flatnose 14/40 (1927-29), the 18/80 Mark I and II (1928-30), and the Tigress 18/100 Mark III (1930-31). Contact: David Potter, Tinkers Revel, Woodham Walter, Maldon, Essex CM9 6RJ, England. Phone: 011-44-245-225-167.

MMM (or Triple-M) Register: For the overhead cam Midgets (1929-36), Magnas (1931-33), and Magnettes (1932-36). Contact: Jackie Hayter, 49 Breach Avenue, Southbourne, Ernsworth, Hants PO16 8NB, England. Phone: 011-44-243-371-440.

SVW Register: For large sedans and tourers SA (1936-39), VA (1937-39), and WA (1939). Contact: David Washburn, Firswood, High Park Avenue, East Horsley, Leatherhead, Surrey KT24 5DF, England.

T Register: For the TA (1936-39), TB (1939), TC (1945-50), TD (1950-53), and TF (1953-55). Contact: David Barnes, 18 Eaton Rise, Ealing, London W5 2ER, England. Phone: 011-44-81-997-0118.

Y Type Register: For the four-seater sedans and tourer with XPAG engines (1947-53). Contact: Dennis Doubtfire, Eden House, Portsmouth Road, Milford, Dodalming, Surrey GU8 5DS, England.

Z Magnette Register: For the ZA (1953-56), ZB (1956-58), Mark III and Mark IV (1959-68). Contact: Paul Batho, 2 Church St., Cottages, Upyon, Oxon OX11 9JB, England. Phone: 011-44-235-850-488.

MGA Register: For roadsters and coupes with the B series engine (1955-1962). Contact: Geoff Barton, "Oak Lea," Burleigh Road, Ascot, Berks SL5 7PA, England.

MGA Twin Cam Register: For the MGA with the double overhead cam engine (1958-1960). Contact: Nick Cox, 15 Orchard Drive, Wooburn Green, Bucks HP10 0QN, England.

MGB Register: For the 1.8-liter roadsters and GTs. Contact: Don Bishop, 28 Freegrounds Road, Hedge End, Southampton, Hants SO3 4HR, England. Phone: 011-44-489-782-876.

MGC Register: For the 3-liter, 6-cylinder roadsters and GTs (1967-69). Contact: Bob Dixon, 43 Arnolds Crescent, Newbold Verdon, Leics LE9 9LD, England. Phone 011-44-455-823-833.

V-8 Register: For the 3.5-liter GT with the Rover V-8 engine (1972-76) and the RV-8 (1993 to date). Contact: Gavin Bailey, 165 Victoria Road, London N22 4XH, England. Phone: 011-44-81-889-4769.

Midget Register: For the 950, 1100, 1275, and 1500 models (1961-79). Contact: Graeme Hall, 27 Alexandra Street, Burton Latimer, Kettering NN15 5SE, England. Phone: 011-44-799-513-730.

FWD Register: For the 1100 and 1300 (1962-70), MG Metro and 6R4 (1982-91), Maestro and Montego (1984-91). Contact: Peter Green, 5 Dukes Close, Kings Road, Alton, Hants GU34 1PH, England. Phone: 011-44-420-89339.

MGF Register: For the mid-engined two-seater built by Rover Cars (1995 to date). Contact: Julia Marshall, 82a Chesil Street, Winchester, Hants SO23 0HX, England. Phone: 011-44-962-771-722 or work 011-44-962-854-117.

MGCC U.S. and Canadian Centers

Overseas Director: John Hale, "Beech Garth," Partan Road, Churchdown, Glouchestershire GL3 2JH, England. Phone: 011-44-452-856-825.

North and South America Director: Nick Cox, Wooburn Green, Bucks HP10 0QN, England. Phone: 011-44-628-533-149.

MG Car Club of Toronto: Contact Keith Holdsworth, PO Box 64, Station R, Toronto, Ontario, Canada M4G 3Z3. Phone: 416-533-MGMG. E-mail: holdswo@io.org.

MG Owners: Contact George Steneberg Jr., 9 Pomona Avenue, El Cerrito, CA 94530.

Sacramento Valley MG Car Club: Contact Corey Hogue, PO Box 2511, Fair Oaks, CA 95628.

Vintage MG Club of Southern California: Contact Raymond Temple, 5191 Chablis Circle, Irvine, CA 92714.

Long Beach MG Car Club: Write PO Box 1727, Long Beach, CA 90801.

Abingdon Rough Riders: Contact A.J. Chalmers, 1231 12th Avenue, San Francisco, CA 94122.

TC Motoring Guild: Write The Secretary, PO Box 3452, Van Nuys, CA 91407.

Rocky Mountain Centre MG Car Club: Contact Jay Nemeth-Johannes, PO Box 152, Denver, CO 80201. E-mail: jayj@lvld.hp.com.

Connecticut MG Club Ltd: Contact A.L. Heady, 65 Pumpkin Hill Road, New Milford, CT 06776. Phone: 203-647-1385.

Southern Connecticut MG Car Club: Contact Joanne Raymond, 12 Old Redding Road, West Redding, CT 06896.

Florida MG Car Club: Contact Jerome P. Keuper, PO Box 394, Melbourne Beach, FL 32951.

Florida Suncoast MG Car Club: Write PO Box 0251, Tampa, FL 33601-0251.

Peachtree MG Registry Ltd: Contact Kevin Walsh, 344 Cadwell Rd., North Covington, GA 30209. Phone: 404-787-3030.

Chicagoland MGB Club: Contact James Evans, PO Box 455, Addison, IL 60101.

MGs of Baltimore: Contact Richard D. Liddick, 7200 Park Drive, Baltimore, MD 21234-7023. Phone: 410-882-6896. E-mail: RGL2MGBGT@aol.com.

West Michigan "OSH" MG Car Club: Contact John E. Leese, 2129 Deer Hollow Dr. SE, Grand Rapids, MI 49508.

Windsor-Detroit MG Car Club: Contact Dan Bebaran, 1327 Austin, Lincoln Park, MI 48146-2002. Phone: 313-382-6715.

MG Club of St. Louis: Write 1326 Weldon Avenue, St. Louis, MO 63130.

Metrolina MG Car Club: Write 320 Harvard Drive, Albermarle, NC 28001.

North Carolina MG Car Club: Contact Bill Hawkins, PO Box 72273, Raleigh, NC 27605.

MG Car Club Central Jersey Centre: Write PO Box 435, Convent Station, NJ 07961.

Eastern New York MGA Club: Contact Ray Schwarz, 3B Shadyside Avenue, South Nyack, NY 10960. Phone: 914-358-8247.

Western New York MG Car Club: Contact George R. Herschell, 1286 Mill Creek Run, Webster, NY 14580.

Emerald Necklace MG Register: Write PO Box 81152, Cleveland, OH 44181.

South Western Ohio MG Car Club: Write PO Box 32, Dabel Branch, Dayton, OH 45420.

Keystone MG Car Club: Contact George Iacocca, 1040 Miriam Drive, Emmaus, PA 18049.

British Motorcar Owners Club SE: Contact William W. Sapp, PO Box 1274, Gramling, SC 29438.

Houston MG Car Club: Write MG Car Club, PO Box 441-1241, Houston, TX 77244-1241.

Texas MG Register: Write 15 Cimarron Trail, Lucas, TX 75002.

Washington DC MG Car Club: Write PO Box 6321, Arlington, VA 22206.

MG Car Club NorthWest Center: Contact Membership Chairman, PO Box 84284, Seattle, WA 98124-5584. Phone: 206-362-8681. E-mail mgccnwc@eskimo.com.

Milwaukee Great Lakes MG Motorcar Group: Contact Wayne F. Chandler, 11713 W. Oxford Place, Milwaukee, WI 53226.

North American MMM Register

Like its British counterpart, the North American Triple M Register is for owners of overhead cam Midgets from 1929-36, Magnas from 1931-33, and Magnettes from 1932-36. Contact: Tom Metcalf, Registrar, 1532 St. Rt. 60 South, Ashland, OH 44805. Phone: 419-289-6241.

New England MG T Register

Founded in 1964, the New England MG T Register has more than 4,500 members and 40 local chapters in the United States and Canada. The group is dedicated to the maintenance, preservation, and enjoyment of the T-series cars. It publishes a bimonthly magazine, *The Sacred Octagon*, that is packed with articles, photographs, drawings, technical information, spare parts information, ads, and other materials of interest to MG T owners.

The T Register holds two annual meetings, both called Gathering of the Faithful, or GOF. The GOF is informal, low-pressure, and social oriented. A GOF will consist of photo contests, model displays, gymkhanas, rallies, and car displays.

Three levels of membership are available. Full membership is for owners of T-Types, Y-Types, and other variations as long as they are powered by engines of that era. Vintage membership is for owners of pre-1940, non-T-Type cars. Associate membership is for anyone who loves MGs.

For information, write MG, Drawer 220, Oneonta, NY 13820.

The New York/Connecticut Chapter of the NEMGTR may be contacted by writing 4 The Circle, Warwick, NY 10990.

The South Eastern MG T-Register contact is Don Harmer, 3926 Harts Mill Lane, Atlanta, GA 30319.

MGA Registers

Naturally catering to owners of MGAs, the MGA Register began in October 1970 in England. It publishes a bimonthly magazine, *MGActivities*, that is available from the publishers, Snowball Press, 14a Cross Street, Reading, Berkshire RG1 1SN, England.

Membership information for the Register may be obtained by writing the Register Chairman, 12 Sweet Briar Clough, Rochdale, Lancs OL21 6NX, England.

A North American MGA Register also exists, having been organized in the summer of 1975. The NAMGAR has over 3,200 MGAs registered in North America and throughout the world. The club publishes a bimonthly newsletter, MGA!, with technical, historic, and general-interest information for MGA enthusiasts. The club sponsors Get Togethers around the country.

For membership information, contact Len Bonnay, 538 Alan Avenue, Welland, Ontario, Canada L3C 2Y9. E-mail: NAMGARUSA@aol.com.

MGA Twin Cam Group

A subset of the MGA registers is the MGA Twin Cam Group, organized in 1965 by Mike Ellman-Brown, who is recorded as purchasing the last MGA Twin Cam. Membership is in the hundreds, but the Group has succeeded in registering more than 6,000 Twin Cams around the world. Since these cars are fussy and tend to have engines that are unlike any other MG engine, it is the group to contact for information on these cars.

Membership information may be obtained from the General Secretary, 9 Grenville Way, Shitley Bay, Tyne & Wear NE26 3JJ, England.

The U.S. Twin Cam Registry is based in Indiana. Contact: Lyle York, 5105 Kingswood Lane, Anderson, IN 46011.

American MGB Association

Founded in 1975, the American MGB Association is the official registry for MGBs, MGB/GTs, and MG Midgets in North America. AMGBA has more than 2,000 members in North America and worldwide. AMGBA publishes a quarterly magazine, *The Octagon*, that contains technical information, articles, and photographs from AMGBA members.

The club holds an annual convention in a different city of the United States each year. The convention attracts MGs from all over North America for an informal weekend of fun and camaraderie. Regional conventions are also held throughout the country.

For information, contact The American MGB Association, PO Box 11401, Chicago, IL 60611. Their phone number is 312-843-3898.

North American MGB Register

The principal MGB group in the world and the best to obtain information on V-8-powered cars. Founded in 1990, the NAMGBR covers the entire country. Every other month the club publishes a magazine devoted to the MGB that is packed with news and maintenance tips.

For membership information, write North American MGB Register, PO Box MGB, Akin, IL 62805. Phone: 800-626-4271, or 618-439-6464.

American MGC Register

Owners of MGCs in North America have their own Register dedicated to them. Contact: Tom Boscarino, 34 Park Avenue, Asheville, NC 28803-2056. Phone: 704-274-2269.

MG Owners' Club

This club was founded in 1973, and is Britain's largest club with more than 50,000 members. This club caters more to Midget, MGB, MGC, and V-8 owners and fans.

The MG Owners' Club has a publication, *Enjoying MG*, that is a source of cars for sale and low-cost insurance and is one of the club's strengths. As with the MG Car Club, events held in Britain tend to be large, with a wide variety of cars.

For membership information, contact the Membership Secretary, Octagon House, Station Road, Swavesey, Cambridge CB4 5QZ, England. The phone number (if dialing from the United States) is 011-44-954-231-125. The fax number is 011-44-954-232-106.

The club also has a web site on the Internet: http://www.mgcars.org.uk/mgoc.

MG Vintage Racers

This organization is for those people interested in vintage racing their MGs (as opposed to full-bore racing of the cars). Vintage racing generally involves nonbody-contact competition, although accidents do happen.

Contact Mark Palmer, 253 Bridle Path Road, Bethlehem, PA 18017 for additional information. His phone number is 610-867-6014 and his fax is 610-954-9489.

Internet

As with almost every other organization in the world today, the MG Car Club and MG Owners' Club are both on the Internet. To get information on either club, you can search for "MG Car Club" or go to http://www.mgcars.org.uk for probably more information than you'd ever want about MGs. The site includes information about the individual clubs and the international clubs, and has contact lists for additional information. There's also a way to join the clubs on the 'net. There is information at that site on detail restoration of MGs, including replacing heaters, suspensions, and windshields. You can also find information on all MG car clubs, registers, and centers if you're interested in joining.

Resource Guide

British Motor Industry Heritage Trust

Anyone contemplating the purchase of an older automobile of any make should be aware of the various sources of parts and information. We hope this Buyer's Guide will at least start you out on the right foot. But any project requiring restoration also requires a resource guide with information on where to find everything, or at least where to go to make the first contact.

Again, the resources listed below have been culled from various references. It is advisable to call ahead to find out if the company is still in business and operating from the same location, and if what they are offering is still the same. While every effort has been made to ensure accuracy, people and companies do move.

The prime resource for all searches on MG must be the British Motor Industry Heritage Trust. Based in the Heritage Motor Centre at Gaydon Warwickshire, the group can trace its roots back to 1975, when Leyland Cars approved the creation of a group called Leyland Historic Vehicles. The name of this group was changed in 1979 to BL Heritage. The Heritage launched an approval scheme in 1980 for companies that specialized in the sale and manufacture of obsolete parts for cars built by BL Cars and its predecessors. More than 50 companies are part of the Association of Heritage Approved Specialists.

In 1983, BL Heritage became more independent and was replaced by the British Motor Industry Heritage Trust, an education trust designed to include all of England's car makers. Soon after the formation, however, Ford and Vauxhall withdrew. After the creation of BMIHT, the parts and approval section came under the control of British Motor Heritage, which was intended to be the cash-generating part of the Trust.

BMH builds bodies for the MG RV8. But more importantly, BMIHT is a source of information on all British cars, particularly MG. Through BMIHT you can obtain literature to help in restoration as well as some of the original sales numbers and such for a particular vehicle, based on registration numbers and serial numbers.

British Motor Industry Heritage Trust
Heritage Motor Centre
Burbury Road
Gaydon, Warwickshire CV35 0B5
England
Phone: 011-44-1926-641-188
Fax: 011-44-1926-641-555

Moss Motors

A second invaluable source of parts and information is Moss Motors. While this isn't necessarily an endorsement, Moss Motors has just about everything you could need to restore or repair your MG (or any British car). Its source of supplies is apparently unlimited, as is the staff's knowledge of repair and replacement. Many Moss replacement parts are Heritage-certified, which gives them the best stamp of approval they could get. Moss Motors also has body and engine parts, as well as those little pieces you may need to make your restoration complete.

The Moss Motors catalog is filled with useful information and data. The MGA catalog, for example, has six diagrams on where to find serial numbers; seven engine diagrams, including three "exploded" views; an "exploded" view of the manifolds and exhaust system; the cooling system; engine and carburetor controls and carburetors (an excellent way to learn how they work); the fuel system; the clutch and transmission; the front suspension and steering; rear axle; the rear suspension and driveshaft; brakes, lines, and brake controls; the chassis and all body parts, including panels. Most of the diagrams are taken from the service manuals, so you know they're authentic.

Moss Motors has catalogs on the T-series, MGA, MGB, and Spridgets, and are free when you stop at the Moss Motors stands at most British car shows, or you can contact Moss Motors directly.

Moss Motors, Ltd.
Eastern Warehouse and Sales Counter
Hamilton Business Park, Unit 4A
Victory Gardens, NJ 07801
201-361-9358

Western Warehouse and Sales Counter
7200 Hollister Avenue
PO Box 847
Goleta, CA 93117
805-968-1041
800-235-6954
Fax: 805-968-6910

London Warehouse and Sales Counter
22-28 Manor Road
Richmond, Surrey TW9 TYB England

There are, obviously, hundreds of sources for British and MG car parts, accessories, and help. Here is a listing of a few of those sources, first in the United States and then in Britain.

United States, General Parts Sources
GP Abingdon Ltd.
129 West Main St.
Tarrytown, NY 10591
Phone: 914-631-7163
Fax: 914-631-7921

Abingdon Spares, Ltd.
PO Box 37
South St.
Walpole, NH 03608
Phone: 603-756-4768
Fax: 603-756-9614

Antique & Classic Car Restoration
Hwy 107, Box 368
Magdalena, NM 87825

Automobile Water Here
7119 E. Shea, Ste. 106265
Scottsdale, AZ 85254
Phone: 602-948-6901

Automotive Artistry
401 E. Streetsboro Rd.
Hudson, OH 44236
Phone: 216-650-1503

Barlow & Co.
7 Maple Ave.
Newton, NH 03858
Phone: 603-382-3591
Fax: 603-382-4406

BCP Sport & Classic Co.
10525 Airline Dr.
Houston, TX 77037
Phone: 713-448-4739
Fax: 713-448-0189

Bob's Foreign Auto Repair
801 Huntington Pike
Rockledge, PA 19046
Phone: 215-663-1343

Bonnets Up
5736 Spring St.
Clinton, MD 20735
Phone: 301-297-4759

Boston MG Shop
40R Griggs St.
Allston, MA 02134
Phone: 617-731-2348

Brit-Tek Ltd.
12 Parmenter Rd.
Londonderry, NH 03053
Phone: 800-255-5883

British Car Specialists
2060 N. Wilson Way
Stockton, CA 95205
Phone: 209-948-8767
Fax: 209-948-1030

British Cars Ltd.
335 Park Ave. E.
Mansfield, OH 44905
Phone: 419-525-1866

British Miles
9278 Old E. Tyburn Rd.
Morrisville, PA 19067
Phone: 215-736-9300
Fax: 215-736-3089

British Motors Ltd.
1427 East Geer St.
Durham, NC 27704
Phone: 919-688-0899

British Motorsports, Inc.
1143 Dell Ave.
Campbell, CA 95008
Phone: 408-370-7174
Fax: 408-370-0240

British Restorations
4455 Paul St.
Philadelphia, PA 19124
Phone: 215-533-6696

British Sports Car Centre Inc.
9505 N. Freeway
Houston, TX 77037
Phone: 800-749-2748
Fax: 713-591-2881

British T Shop Inc.
165 Rt. 82
Oakdale, CT 06370
Phone: 203-889-0178
Fax: 203-889-6096

British Tools and Fasterners
2030 Andre Ave.
Los Osos, CA 93402
Phone: 805-528-0418
Fax: 805-528-0358

British Spares West
5616 Laurel Canyon Blvd.
No. Hollywood, CA 91607
Phone: 800-997-2787
Fax: 818-760-3550

BritParts Midwest
603 Monroe St.
Laporte, IN 46350
Phone: 800-852-5729
Fax: 219-324-7541

Brooklands Inc.
503 Corporate Square
1500 NW 62nd St.
Ft. Lauderdale, FL 33309
Phone: 305-776-2748
Fax: 305-772-8383

Brooklands/MG Only
8235/8237 S. Tacoma Way
Tacoma, WA 98499
Phone: 206-584-2033

CARS
Computer Aided Resale System
28 Bradley Cir.
Hilton Head Island, SC 29928
Phone: 803-785-8533
Fax: 803-842-4500

CARS Corp.
PO Box 2611
Ponte Verde Beach, FL 32004
Phone: 904-285-9447
Fax: 800-860-4227

Checquered Flag International
4128 Lincoln Blvd.
Marina Del Rey, CA
Phone: 310-827-8665
Fax: 310-821-1272

Clarke Spares & Restorations
90 W. Swamp Road
Doylestown, PA 18901
Phone: 215-348-0595
Fax: 215-348-4160

Classic Wood Mfg.
1006 N. Raleigh St.
Greensboro, NC 27405
Phone: 910-691-1344
Fax: 910-273-3074

Doug's British Car Parts
2487 E. Colorado Blvd.
Pasadena, CA 91107
Phone: 818-793-2494
Fax: 818-793-4339

Eberhardt Service
17710 Valley View Ave.
Cleveland, OH 44135-1126

Faspec British Parts
1036 SE Stark St.
Portland, OR 97214
Phone: 503-232-1232
Fax: 503-230-8838

Don Flye
Petersham Rd.
Athol, MA 01331
Phone: 508-724-3318

Geneva Foreign & Sports
401 Hamilton St.
Geneva, NY 14456
Phone: 315-789-4575
Fax: 315-781-2309

Peter Groh Keys
9957 Frederick Rd.
Ellicot City, MD 21042
Phone: 410-750-2352

Liverpool Motor Works
RD1, Box 19B
Liverpool, PA 17045
Phone: 717-444-3773

M&G Vintage Auto
265 Rt. 17, Box 226
Tuxedo Park, NY 10987
Phone: 914-753-5900
Fax: 914-753-5613

MCR Motor Car Racing & Renovations
125-R Old West Lake Rd.
Honeoye, NY 14471
Phone: 716-229-4314

MG COSAS
24027 Crosslands
San Antonio, TX 78264
Phone: 800-846-2672

Mini Motors Classic Coachworks
2775 Cherry Ave. NE
Salem, OR 97303
Phone: 503-362-3187
Fax: 503-375-9609

Motorcars Ltd.
8101 Hempstead
Houston, TX 77008
Phone: 713-863-9388
Fax: 713-863-8238

Motormetrics
5500 Thomaston Rd.
Macon, GA 31204
Phone: 912-477-6771

Mr. Sports Car Inc.
203 E. Lincoln
Papillon, NE 68046
Phone: 402-592-7559

Northwest Import Parts
10042 S.W. Balmer, Dept. 7
Portland, OR 97219
Phone: 503-245-3806
Fax: 503-245-9617

O'Connor Classic Autos
2569 Scott Blvd.
Santa Clara, CA 95050
Phone: 408-727-0430
Fax: 408-727-3987

Omni Specialties
10418 Lorain Ave.
Cleveland, OH 44111
Phone: 216-251-2269
Fax: 216-251-6083

Pacific International Auto
1118 Garnet Ave.
San Diego, CA 92109
Phone: 619-274-1920
Fax: 619-454-1815

Pearson's British Cars
745 Orange Ave.
Winter Park, FL 32789
Phone: 407-647-0967

Peninsula Imports
3749 Harlem Rd.
Buffalo, NY 14215
Phone: 800-263-4538
Fax: 905-847-3021

Porter Service & Restoration
HG84, Box 64
Keyser, WV 26726
Phone: 304-788-5199

Quality Coaches
20 W. 38th St.
Minneapolit, MN 55409
Phone: 612-824-4155

The Roadster Factory
PO Box 332
Armagh, PA 15920
Phone: 800-234-1104

Service Consultants
South Rd.
Deerfield, NH 03037
Phone: 603-463-8816

Shadetree Motors Ltd.
3895 Mammoth Cave Ct.
Pleasanton, CA 94588
Phone: 510-846-1309

Special Interest Car Parts
1340 Hartford Ave.
Johnston, RI 02919
Phone: 800-851-5600
Phone: 401-831-8850
Fax: 401-831-7760

Sports & Classics
PO Box 1787
512 Boston Post Road
Darien, CT 06820-1787

Tiger Detailing
PO Box 9875
North Hollywood, CA 91609-1875
Phone: 818-982-1042

University Motors Ltd.
6490 E. Fulton
Ada, MI 49301
Phone: 616-682-0800
Fax: 616-682-0801

V6 MGB
Box 741992
Dallas, TX 75374

Victoria British Ltd.
PO Box 14991
Lenexa, KS 66285
Phone: 800-255-0088
Phone: 913-541-8500
Fax: 913-599-3299

Vintage Racing Services, Inc.
1785 Barnum Ave.
Stratford, CT 06497
Phone: 203-386-1736
Fax: 203-386-0486

Web Accessories
PO Box 191
Old Bethpage, NY 11804
Phone: 516-752-1710

West Coast Street Rods
11470 Vanowen St.
North Hollywood, CA 91605
Phone: 818-982-2220

Brakes
Stainless Steel Brakes Corp.
11470 Main Road
Clarence, NY 14031
Phone: 800-448-7722
Phone: 716-759-8666
Fax: 716-759-8688

Apple Hydraulics
1610 Middle Rd.
Calverton, NY 11933
Phone: 800-882-7753
Phone: 516-369-9515
Fax: 516-369-9516

White Post Restorations
One Old Car Drive
White Post, VA 22663
Phone: 540-837-1140

Sierra Specialty Automotive
3494 Chandler Rd.
Quincy, CA 95971
Phone: 800-427-2771

Electrical

American-Foreign Auto Electric, Inc.
103 Main St.
Souderton, PA 18964
Phone: 215-723-4877

British Wiring, Inc.
20449 Ithaca
Olympia Fields, IL 60461
Phone: 708-481-9050

Palo Alto Speedometer Inc.
718 Emerson St.
Palo Alto, CA 94301
Phone: 415-323-0243
Fax: 415-323-4632

Engines

University Motors Ltd.
6940 East Fulton St.
Ada, MI 49301
Phone: 616-682-0800
Fax: 616-682-0801

Sports Car International
6405 Cochiti SE
Albuquerque, NM 87108
Phone: 505-268-6898
Fax: 505-232-3551

Joe Curto Carburetors
22-09 126 St.
College Point, NY 11356
Phone: 718-762-7878
Fax: 718-762-6287

Reference Material

Motorbooks International
PO Box 1
Osceola, WI 54020
Phone: 800-458-0454

British Car Bookshop
PO Box 1683
Los Altos, CA 94203
Phone: 800-520-8292
Phone: 415-949-9680
Fax: 415-949-9685

Britbooks
62 Main St.
Otego, NY 13825
Phone: 607-988-7956

MG MMM Register Library
Knowle House, Hooke Road
East Horsley, Leatherhead
Surrey KT24 5DY, England

Steering Wheels

Lecarra Steering Wheels
15850 W. 6th Ave.
Golden, CO 80401
Phone: 800-432-8170

Tops and Seals

Dave's Interior Restorations
525 Chestnut Street
Emmaus, PA 18049
Phone: 610-965-2172
Fax: 610-967-2672

The Roadster Factory
PO Box 332
Killen Road
Armagh, PA 15920
Phone: 800-678-8764
Fax: 814-446-6729

Ragtops and Roadsters
203 S. 4th St.
Perkasie, PA 18944
Phone: 215-257-1202

Transmissions

Rivergate Restoration Products
11703 Rivergate Bay Lane
Soddy, TN 37379

Wheels and Tires

K-Speed Inc.
3015 Research Drive
State College, PA 16801
Phone: 800-494-0708

British Sources

M&G International
International House
Lord Street, Birkenhead L4 1HT
England
Phone: 011-44-51-666-1666
Fax: 011-44-51-666-2123

MG Parts Centre (prewar)
1A Albany Road
Chislehurst
Kent BR7 6BG England
Phone: 011-44-1-467-7788
Fax: 011-44-1-295-1277

Moss Europe Ltd.
Unit 15 Allington Way
Yarm Road Ind. Estate, Darlington
Co. Durham DL1 4QB, England
Phone: 011-44-325-281-343
Fax: 011-44-325-485-563

John Skinner Manufacturing Ltd.
82B Chesterton Lane
Cirencester, Glos GL7 1YD, England
Phone: 011-44-285-657-410
Fax: 011-44-285-650-013

Vintage Restorations
The Old Bakery
Windmill Street
Tunbridge Wells, Kent TN2 4UU, England
Phone: 011-44-892-525-899
Fax: 011-44-892-525-499

The MGB Hive
011-44-945-700-500
Fax: 011-44-945-700-130

Simon Robinson Classics
Ketton Garage, Durham Road
Coatham, Munderville, Darlington DL1
3LZ, England
Phone: 011-44-325-311-232
Fax: 011-44-325-317-952

The Hutson Motor Company Ltd.
Pawson Street
Bradford, W. Yorkshire BD4 8DF
England
Phone: 011-44-274-669-052
Fax: 011-44-274-669-685

NTG Motor Services Ltd.
282-284 Bramford Road
Ipswich IP1 4AY, England
Phone: 011-44-473-211-240
Fax: 011-44-473-743-133

Peter Rees Wheels
Phone: 011-44-342-850-551

The Pre-War MG Parts Centre
1A Albany Road
Chislehurst, Kent BR7 6BG
England
Phone: 011-44-81-467-7788
Fax: 011-44-81-295-1277

Batheaston Atrefactors
Comfortable Place
Upper Bristol Road, Bath BA1 3AJ
England
Phone: 011-44-225-482-737
Fax: 011-44-225-482-265

Naylor Brothers
Regent House
Dockfield Road, Shipley, W. Yorks BD17 7SF, England
Phone: 011-44-274-594-071
Fax: 011-44-274-531-149

Prestife Auto Trim Products Ltd.
3 Prenton Way
North Cheshire Trading Estate
Birkenhead L43 3DU, England
Phone: 011-44-51-608-8683
Fax: 011-44-51-608-0439

Frontline Developments
Unit 1, Venture House
Melcombe Road, Oldfield Park, Bath BA2 3LR, England
Phone: 011-44-225-446-544

Romney Shields MG Parts Centre
25 Rutherford Close, Progress Road
Eastwood Industrial Estate, Leigh-on-Sea, Essex
SS9 5LQ, England
Phone: 011-44-702-529-070

British Sports Car Spares
301 Goldharwk Road
London W12 8EZ, England
Phone: 011-44-81-748-7823
Fax: 011-44-81-563-0101

The Welsh MG Centre
Pen-Y-Bryn
Wrexham, Clwyd
North Wales
Phone: 011-44-978-263-445
Fax: 011-44-978-351-635

A Smattering of Museums

MGs are featured in several North American automobile museums. Primary among these is the Westminster MG Car Museum in Westminster, Vermont.

Among the more than 29 models on display is a 1927 14/28 Tourer Flatnose four-seater, one of only six known to exist and one of the oldest MGs in the United States. The museum also has a 1930 M-Type Sportsman's Coupe, one of only three known to exist; a 1933 J-4 Supercharged Racer; a 1938 SA four-door Tourer with a Charelesworth body; an 1953 TD four-seater, one of four built; the 1955 EX182 MGA prototype; and a 1964 Mark IV Magnette, as well as a 1934 PB Airline Coupe and a TC. The museum is open daily in July and August.

The Henry Ford Museum and Greenfield Village in Dearborn, Michigan, has an MGTC on display among its hundreds of cars. This museum is open daily and is worth the trip for the variety of automobiles and other objects on display.

The Gast Classic Motorcar Museum in Strasburg, Pennsylvania, has on display the first MG imported to the United States, a 1929 M-Type, and the last, a 1980 MGB Limited Edition Roadster. The M-Type was purchased new by Edsel Ford, son of Henry I; the MGB was purchased by Henry Ford II, son of Edsel.

Magazines

British Car
PO Box 1653
Los Altos, CA 94022
Phone: 415-949-9680
Fax: 415-949-9685
Subscription: $22.95/year

Classic & Sportscar
Haymarket Magazines Ltd.
60 Waldegrove Road
Teddington, Middlesex TW11 8LG
England
Phone: 011-44-81-943-5000
Fax: 011-44-81-943-5844
Subscription: $49/year

Classic Cars
Freepost CY1061
Haywards Heath
West Sussex RH16 3ZA
England
Subscription: $36/yr airfreight to USA

Bibliography

MGA: A History & Restoration Guide. Robert P. Vitrikas. Scarborough Faire, Pawtucket R.I. , 1980.

MGB: The Illustrated History. Jonathan Wood and Lionel Burrell. Haynes Publishing, Somerset, 1994.

MG: The Magic of the Marque. Mike Allison. Dalton Watson, London, 1989.

MG by McComb. F. Wilson McComb. Osprey Publishing, London, 1990.

MG V-8: Twenty-one Years on . . . From Introduction to RV-8. David Knowles and the MG Car Club V-8 Register. Windrow & Greene.

Standard Catalog of Imported Cars. James M. Flammang. Krause Publications, Inc., 1992.

The Enthusiast's Guide to British Postwar Classic Cars. Jonathan Wood, Osprey Publishing, London, 1980.

Index